Nanotechnology

Other Books of Related Interest:

At Issue series

Designer Babies

Drones

Embryonic and Adult Stem Cells

Introducing Issues with Opposing Viewpoints

Stem Cell Research

Opposing Viewpoints series

Human Genetics

Robotic Technology

"Congress shall make no law . . . abridging the freedom of speech, or of the press."

First Amendment to the US Constitution

The basic foundation of our democracy is the First Amendment guarantee of freedom of expression. The Opposing Viewpoints series is dedicated to the concept of this basic freedom and the idea that it is more important to practice it than to enshrine it.

Nanotechnology

Noah Berlatsky, Book Editor

GREENHAVEN PRESS
A part of Gale, Cengage Learning

Farmington Hills, Mich • San Francisco • New York • Waterville, Maine
Meriden, Conn • Mason, Ohio • Chicago

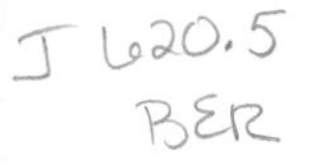

Elizabeth Des Chenes, *Director, Content Strategy*
Cynthia Sanner, *Publisher*
Douglas Dentino, *Manager, New Product*

WCN: 01-100-101

For more information, contact:
Greenhaven Press
27500 Drake Rd.
Farmington Hills, MI 48331-3535
Or you can visit our Internet site at gale.cengage.com

Articles in Greenhaven Press anthologies are often edited for length to meet page requirements. In addition, original titles of these works are changed to clearly present the main thesis and to explicitly indicate the author's opinion. Every effort is made to ensure that Greenhaven Press accurately reflects the original intent of the authors. Every effort has been made to trace the owners of copyrighted material.

LIBRARY OF CONGRESS CATALOGING-IN-PUBLICATION DATA

Nanotechnology / Noah Berlatsky, book editor.
pages cm. -- (Opposing viewpoints)
Summary: "This title addresses various issues related to nanotechnology, including what the relationship between public perception and nanotechnology is, how nanotechnology will affect health, how nanotechnology will affect the environment, and how nanotechnology will affect international relations"-- Provided by publisher.
Includes bibliographical references and index.
ISBN 978-0-7377-6961-6 (hardback) -- ISBN 978-0-7377-6962-3 (paperback)
1. Nanotechnology I. Berlatsky, Noah, editor of compilation.
T174.7.N345525 2014
620'.5--dc23

2013036318

Printed in the United States of America
1 2 3 4 5 6 7 18 17 16 15 14

Contents

Why Consider Opposing Viewpoints?

> *"The only way in which a human being can make some approach to knowing the whole of a subject is by hearing what can be said about it by persons of every variety of opinion and studying all modes in which it can be looked at by every character of mind. No wise man ever acquired his wisdom in any mode but this."*
>
> *John Stuart Mill*

In our media-intensive culture it is not difficult to find differing opinions. Thousands of newspapers and magazines and dozens of radio and television talk shows resound with differing points of view. The difficulty lies in deciding which opinion to agree with and which "experts" seem the most credible. The more inundated we become with differing opinions and claims, the more essential it is to hone critical reading and thinking skills to evaluate these ideas. Opposing Viewpoints books address this problem directly by presenting stimulating debates that can be used to enhance and teach these skills. The varied opinions contained in each book examine many different aspects of a single issue. While examining these conveniently edited opposing views, readers can develop critical thinking skills such as the ability to compare and contrast authors' credibility, facts, argumentation styles, use of persuasive techniques, and other stylistic tools. In short, the Opposing Viewpoints Series is an ideal way to attain the higher-level thinking and reading skills so essential in a culture of diverse and contradictory opinions.

In addition to providing a tool for critical thinking, Opposing Viewpoints books challenge readers to question their own strongly held opinions and assumptions. Most people form their opinions on the basis of upbringing, peer pressure, and personal, cultural, or professional bias. By reading carefully balanced opposing views, readers must directly confront new ideas as well as the opinions of those with whom they disagree. This is not to argue simplistically that everyone who reads opposing views will—or should—change his or her opinion. Instead, the series enhances readers' understanding of their own views by encouraging confrontation with opposing ideas. Careful examination of others' views can lead to the readers' understanding of the logical inconsistencies in their own opinions, perspective on why they hold an opinion, and the consideration of the possibility that their opinion requires further evaluation.

Evaluating Other Opinions

To ensure that this type of examination occurs, Opposing Viewpoints books present all types of opinions. Prominent spokespeople on different sides of each issue as well as well-known professionals from many disciplines challenge the reader. An additional goal of the series is to provide a forum for other, less known, or even unpopular viewpoints. The opinion of an ordinary person who has had to make the decision to cut off life support from a terminally ill relative, for example, may be just as valuable and provide just as much insight as a medical ethicist's professional opinion. The editors have two additional purposes in including these less known views. One, the editors encourage readers to respect others' opinions—even when not enhanced by professional credibility. It is only by reading or listening to and objectively evaluating others' ideas that one can determine whether they are worthy of consideration. Two, the inclusion of such viewpoints encourages the important critical thinking skill of objectively evaluating an author's credentials and bias. This evaluation will illuminate an author's reasons for taking a particular stance on an issue and will aid in readers' evaluation of the author's ideas.

It is our hope that these books will give readers a deeper understanding of the issues debated and an appreciation of the complexity of even seemingly simple issues when good and honest people disagree. This awareness is particularly important in a democratic society such as ours in which people enter into public debate to determine the common good. Those with whom one disagrees should not be regarded as enemies but rather as people whose views deserve careful examination and may shed light on one's own.

Thomas Jefferson once said that "difference of opinion leads to inquiry, and inquiry to truth." Jefferson, a broadly educated man, argued that "if a nation expects to be ignorant and free . . . it expects what never was and never will be." As individuals and as a nation, it is imperative that we consider the opinions of others and examine them with skill and discernment. The Opposing Viewpoints series is intended to help readers achieve this goal.

David L. Bender and Bruno Leone,
Founders

Introduction

> *"How will life on Earth end? International nuclear bombardment? Another asteroid? Enslavement by aliens? The devouring of all of our resources by a Skynet-esque batch of self-replicating microscopic robots?"*
>
> —*Keith Veronese, "When the World Ends Will You Be Covered in Grey Goo?," io9, September 5, 2011 http://io9.com*

Imagine billions of tiny submicroscopic robots building billions of other tiny submicroscopic robots. In order to get the power they need to keep self-replicating, the robots consume protons, neutrons, atoms—the very building blocks of matter. As the robots eat more and more, there is less and less of everything else, until reality itself collapses into—grey goo!

"Grey goo", and the apocalyptic scenario above, were both first imagined by scientist Eric Drexler in his 1986 book *Engines of Creation*. Drexler worried that self-replicating nanorobots might "replicate swiftly, and reduce the biosphere to dust in a matter of days." He used the term "grey goo" not because the nanorobots would necessarily be grey or gooey but to emphasize that "replicators able to obliterate life might be less inspiring than a single species of crabgrass. They might be 'superior' in an evolutionary sense, but this need not make them valuable."

Grey goo has become a popular trope in apocalyptic science fiction stories. For example, grey-goo-like disasters feature in the 2008 remake of the film *The Day The Earth Stood Still*, in the 2002 Michael Crichton novel *Prey*, and in the Grant Morrison–written comic *The Invisibles* (1994–2000).

So is there a real danger that nanorobots will devour reality and destroy us all? The short answer is no. Drexler himself has largely repudiated the scenario. As quoted by Paul Rincon in a June 9, 2004, article at the BBC website, Drexler said he had "underestimated the popularity of depictions of swarms of tiny nanobugs in science fiction and popular culture." Drexler continues to believe that the grey-goo scenario and self-replicating nanomachines are theoretically physically possible. But he points out that there is no reason to believe that scientists would develop such machines. Even if scientists did create self-replicating machines, he argues, it would be most efficient to control their reproduction from an external computer, and such carefully regulated growth would never lead to a grey-goo apocalypse.

Others have been even more skeptical of the grey-goo scenario. Alok Jha, in a May 25, 2011, article in the *Guardian*, said that a grey-goo apocalypse was "highly improbable" since replicating nanobots would require huge amounts of energy and generate massive heat, making them easy to detect and defuse. Tim Radford in a March 12, 2008, article for the *Guardian*, pointed out that "no one knows how to make this kind of artificial life." Since we do not know how to make self-replicating machines, and don't seem likely to be able to develop them anytime soon, the fear of an imminent grey-goo apocalypse seems overblown.

J. Storrs Hall, the president of the nanotech think tank the Foresight Institute, also argued that grey goo is very, very unlikely. As quoted by Amos Zeeberg in a May 18, 2009, blog post on the *Discover* website, Hall points out that any efficient nanorobot, like any other machine, would be dependent on humans for repair and specialized fuel. "Imagine trying to build a car that ran on hay which it harvested itself, graded its own roads, made its own parts with which it repaired itself, and built new cars," Hall said. "Plagues of nanorobots are about as likely as plagues of hay-eating cars."

While grey goo is not a real danger, it has become an important touchstone, or shorthand, in the debate over nanotechnology. Those who worry about the effects of nanotechnology may mention grey goo as a way to point to worst-case scenarios and unexpected dangers. Those who support nanotechnology research, on the other hand, sometimes point to grey goo to show that fears of nanotechnology can be exaggerated and overblown. Thus, when Prince Charles of Britain raised concerns about the direction of nanotechnology research, he was careful to distance himself from the idea of grey goo. "I do not believe that self-replicating robots, smaller than viruses, will one day multiply uncontrollably and devour our planet," he is quoted as saying in a July 11, 2004, article on the BBC News website. Nonetheless, he said, even if the world is not going to dissolve into grey goo, it is important to "ensure that proper attention is given to the risks" and the potential downsides of nanotechnology.

Grey goo is an extreme and imaginative idea, but nanotechnology has real potential benefits as well as real potential dangers. The authors in this book debate these possibilities in chapters titled What Is the Relationship Between Public Perceptions and Nanotechnology?, How Will Nanotechnology Affect Health?, How Will Nanotechnology Affect the Environment?, and How Will Nanotechnology Affect International Relations? Nanotechnology will not destroy the world, but, as the viewpoints here show, it may change it, for better and for worse.

Chapter 1

What Is The Relationship Between Public Perception and Nanotechnology?

Chapter Preface

Ideally, people's understanding of nanotechnology would be shaped by facts and accurate information. Nanotechnology has great potential to change the world for the better; it also has the potential to create health and environmental risks. The public needs to balance these risks and benefits and make informed decisions about how and when nanotechnology should be regulated or promoted.

Unfortunately, accurate information on this issue can be difficult to come by. Worse, recent research shows that in some cases, even accurate information can in certain situations be scrambled and result in misperception and confusion.

A study by the University of Wisconsin tried to find out how readers were affected by trolls—online negative, deliberately confrontational commenters. The researchers showed study participants an article about silver nanoparticles. One group of participants was then shown comments on the article that were negative but civil—for example, one comment said: "Well I think the risks of this technology are just too high for the fish and other plants and animals in water tainted with silver." Another group of participants were shown comments that were negative and rude. For example, "You're stupid if you're not thinking of the risks for the fish and other plants and animals in water tainted with silver."

The researchers, led by Dominique Brossard, found that the negative, rude comments tended to harden and polarize opinions. People who were skeptical about nanotechnology became even more skeptical and suspicious. And people who tended to favor nanotechnology also became more convinced of the rightness of their position.

The research findings present a problem for science journalists and for scientists. You can present information as accurately and carefully and in as balanced a manner as you can in an effort to inform the public, but if comments are open, people are going to be able to say whatever they want—and often what they say will be inaccurate, unbalanced, and incendiary. Worse, reading inflammatory comments is likely to make everyone else respond emotionally and angrily. Rather than thinking about new information and adjusting opinions in light of it, troll comments tend to make people just cling more tightly to their original opinions. "Internet trolls, it seems, negatively frame the science-based debates we see online," Rachel Ehrenberg writes in a March 12, 2013, article in *Science News*. "Their rancor turns what ought to be open-minded considerations of the facts into ad hominem shouting matches among antisocial dwellers beneath bridges."

So what can scientists or journalists or the public do to try to create a better climate for discussing and evaluating scientific issues? Chris Mooney, in a January 19, 2013, article in *Mother Jones*, suggests that scientific understanding might be improved if people just did not read comments on science articles. Perhaps, too, some science sites might consider eliminating comments or moderating them strictly so as to remove trolls or rude remarks. Otherwise, left to themselves, the Wisconsin study suggests, trolls will make us all less informed.

The viewpoints in this chapter debate what other factors influence public perception of nanotechnology, as well as some ways in which public opinion can affect nanotechnology policy and nanotechnology research.

Viewpoint 1

> *"Will [nanotechnology] 'unleash the fire of enlightenment and knowledge or the winds of chaos?'"*

Nanotechnology's Popularity in Science Fiction Suggests That It Can Change the World

Art Molella

Art Molella is the director of the Lemelson Center for the Study of Invention and Innovation. In the following viewpoint, he and the Lemelsons discusss several science fiction scenarios involving nanotechnology, including Michael Crichton's thriller Prey *in which nanomachines swarm together, gain sentience and attack people. Molella contends that this is improbable but suggests that the sci-fi interest in nanotechnology points to the strangeness of nanotechnology and its potentially revolutionary, world-changing implications. Powerful technologies, they conclude, provoke radical and high-flown expectations, even if those expectations may not be fulfilled.*

As you read, consider the following questions:

1. What is self-assembly, according to the author?

Art Molella, "Notes From the Director: In the Nano-World, Anything Can Happen," *Smithsonian*, May 2011.

2. What does Molella say is nanotechnology's holy grail?
3. What activities taught the public about nanotechnology at Spark!Lab in 2011, as reported by the author?

In Michael Crichton's 2002 sci-fi thriller, *Prey*, Jack Forman, a Silicon Valley computer programmer with serious job and marital problems, has been thrust into a military experiment in nanotechnology that has gone haywire. Xymos, a defense contractor in the Nevada desert, has developed molecular-scale cameras that can be injected into the bloodstream to monitor diseases—think *Fantastic Voyage* [a 1966 sci-fi film] without [actress/model] Raquel Welch. The medical application, however, is only a cover for what they are actually making: clouds or "swarms" of tiny nanoscale cameras designed to spy on the enemy.

Sci-Fi Comes True

Jack's wife works for the same top-secret firm, and things quickly get terribly personal for him. But his real problem is trying to bring a runaway technology back under control. It seems that Xymos has magically achieved the fantasy goal of nanotechnology: not only creating molecules by manipulating atoms, but programming atoms to come together on their own, a process known as "self-assembly." The problem is that, once they can self-replicate, these nanoparticles start to behave functionally like living creatures; they don't need humans anymore and anything can happen. Armed with a smidgeon of artificial intelligence, the swarms, so called for their mimicry of the social behavior of bees, are able to learn and evolve with astonishing speed. They go after Jack and anyone who threatens their freedom. The whole world is at peril. Jack wins, but just barely.

Prey ends with some unbelievable death-defying scenes and, for the sake of a good yarn, takes this still-infant technology to implausible extremes, but like the best science fiction writers, the late Crichton could be remarkably prescient about technological breakthroughs, if not their human and social impacts, which are always up for grabs. For example, as I write this, a DARPA [Defense Advanced Research Projects Agency]-funded company is showing off a tiny flying gadget, its so-called Nano Hummingbird, complete with spy video camera—not strictly nano but on the road to it.

A counterbalance to Crichton's dystopian vision is the one given by theoretical physicist Michio Kaku in his new book, *Physics of the Future*. Sensitive to the critiques of nanotechnology, he asks if it will "unleash the fire of enlightenment and knowledge or the winds of chaos?" Kaku looks on the bright side and opts emphatically for the former view; it can and will be controlled, he insists. He then takes us through near, middle, and far future scenarios, based on interviews with working scientists. His examples include super gyroscopes, designer molecules that hunt down cancer cells, DNA "on a chip" that monitors our health, remote-controlled "nanocars" that patrol our bloodstream for cancers (*Fantastic Voyage* again), carbon nanotubes stronger than steel, non-silicon substrates for faster chips and computers, shape-shifting and self-healing structures (think here *Terminator II*), and the nanotechnologist's holy grail, the "replicator" that perhaps by 2100 will manufacture everything at the atomic level practically from nothing, including body organs. The world's major problem will then be the sociopolitical one of learning how to cope with this limitless supply of goods.

Divergent Expectations

History tells us that dawning technologies, especially the more powerful ones, commonly provoke these divergent expectations. In his fascinating new book, *The Information*, James Gleick documents this with technologies from the telegraph and the telephone to the internet. Initial euphoria gives way to

A Sci-Fi Vision of a Sentient Swarm

"So you have a runaway swarm."

"Yes."

"Acting autonomously."

"Yes."

"And this has been going on for . . ."

"Days. About ten days."

"Ten days?" I frowned. "How is that possible, Ricky? The swarm's a collection of micro-robotic machines. Why haven't they decayed, or run out of power? And why exactly can't you control them? Because if they have the ability to swarm, then there's some electrically mediated interaction among them. So you should be able to take control of the swarm—or at least disrupt it."

"All true," Ricky said. "Except we can't. And we've tried everything we can think of." He was focused on the screen, watching intently. "That cloud is independent of us. Period."

Michael Crichton, Prey, *2002.*

fear and anxiety about information overload. But, like Kaku, he puts a positive spin on his subject with some convincing arguments in its favor.

These divergent visions seem particularly pronounced in the case of nanotechnology, even though scientists and engineers have barely scratched the surface of its possibilities. Let me suggest one reason for this. Unlike any other technology to date, nanotechnology operates exclusively in the atomic realm. At the level of the ultra-ultra-small, everything is strange and mysterious. In a 1959 talk titled "There's Plenty of Room at the Bottom," generally recognized as the founding vision for nanotechnology without naming it as such, physicist Richard Feynman described some of the strange, commonsense-defying physics that comes into play. In addition to very short-range electrical forces that cause atoms to hew to one another in strange ways, there are the overriding laws of quantum mechanics that take charge at the nano level. It's a bizarre world of ultimate uncertainty where particles can be in two places and two states at once or even disappear and then reappear someplace else. Feynman once observed that quantum mechanics "describes nature as absurd from the point of view of common sense." A mysterious world indeed, where it seems anything can happen.

It is a measure of the potential and newness of the technology that the public knows of it mainly through fiction and films. To explore today's nano reality, though, we recently participated in NanoDays 2011, a nationwide festival of educational programs about nanoscale science and engineering. In the Lemelson Center's Spark!Lab, our hands-on invention space, visitors of all ages learned about nanotechnology through activities that ranged from measuring their height in nanometers to building a giant model of a carbon nanotube entirely from balloons. At the Lemelson Center, we believe that the tiniest spark of an idea can have widespread impact on everyday life, and with these activities, we sought to fire the imaginations of young people about nanotechnology, without overstating its promises or its dangers.

VIEWPOINT 2

> *"[Real-world nanotechnology] does not sound like the nanotech of science fiction."*

Nanotechnology's Science-Fiction Qualities Have Been Publicly Overhyped

Howard Lovy

Howard Lovy is a Michigan-based writer who specializes in science, business, and innovation. In the following viewpoint, he contends that sci-fi's presentation of the transformational qualities of nanotechnology have been exaggerated, with some damage to the nanotech business. However, he asserts that innovative companies continue to work with nanotechnology in smaller ways by, for example, developing more flame-resistant material. Lovy concludes that there are still business opportunities in nanotechnology for savvy companies who focus on possibilities rather than on hype.

As you read, consider the following questions:

1. According to Lovy, how is nanotech similar to any new technology?

Howard Lovy, "Remember 'Nanotechnology'? It's Still 'Out There', but the Hype Has Gotten Smaller," *Crain's Detroit*, November 9, 2011.

2. What does Lovy say nanotech today has to do with, if not with the quality of the invention?
3. What factors were crucial to the success of T/J Technologies, in the author's opinion?

About a dozen years ago, a wealthy venture capitalist named Rick Snyder launched Ardesta LLC, an Ann Arbor [Michigan] company whose mission was to invest in cutting-edge research in nanotechnology, microsystems and microelectromechanical systems—or MEMS—and bring it to market.

Small Tech

Snyder, the future Michigan governor, coined a new term—"small tech"—to describe the technologies in which he was investing.

It was the turn of the millennium, before [the terrorist attacks on] 9/11, before the Great Recession [of 2008], when the only economic problem on the horizon—potentially—was the Y2K ["year 2000"] computer bug.

The next big thing, as many nanotech promoters said at the time, was going to be very small—100 nanometers or less. For purposes of comparison, a sheet of paper is about 100,000 nanometers thick.

With these tiny, "smart" materials engineered to make products stronger, lighter, faster, the future seemed as if it belonged to a new nanotechnology industry.

Today, however, not too many people in the nano business care to call it an industry at all. It's an enabling technology, and it is developing under the radar in Michigan and elsewhere. This time without the hype.

Ardesta co-founder Chris Rizik recalls that even a decade ago, in the midst of a nanotech investment boom, he and Snyder were a bit wary of that four-letter "nano" prefix. And while the "small tech" they touted did include nanotechnology, it really was not a large part of Ardesta's mission.

"If you take the whole of Ardesta, less than 1 percent of what we did would have been considered nanotechnology," said Rizik, who is now CEO of Renaissance Venture Capital and still runs a scaled-back Ardesta in the governor's absence. "We were believers that it was overhyped even back then. And 10 years ago, there weren't a lot of compelling nanotech products coming out."

Nanotech Bubble

Other venture capitalists and angel [charitable] investors did take stakes in nanotech companies, though. Up until 2005, what was described as a "nanotech bubble" occurred, and many impatient investors lost interest and moved on to other things.

Tim Harper, CEO of the United Kingdom–based nanotech research group Cientifica, estimates that during those peak years, about $300 million was "gambled and lost" on companies making nanomaterials that ultimately would end up being basic commodities "at the bottom end of the value chain."

"It was a classic case of investors jumping in before they fully understood what they were investing in," Harper said.

The thing about nanotech, though, is that it is not unlike any new technology, in that it takes about 15–20 years to make it from lab to marketplace.

Nanotech is still "out there," having continued to develop independent of any investment bubble, Rizik said. It is being used to create advanced materials to make things stronger and lighter or to improve other characteristics.

"And that is really where the more immediate promise of nano was," Rizik said, despite the popular image of "self-replicating nanobots that would form armies to take over the world."

If you ask Gerry Roston, CEO of East Lansing-based In-Pore Technologies, that hype of several years ago is the reason that he is not marketing his Michigan State University [MSU] spinoff as a nanotech company.

InPore makes nanomaterials that, when mixed with other materials, make them stronger, lighter, cheaper and more flame-retardant. But mention the "n" word, and potential customers think of nanoclays—once touted as the "next greatest thing," Roston said. Both Toyota Motor Corp. and General Motors Corp. used them to reinforce parts of their cars.

"There was a lot of hype, a lot of promises, and then it didn't really pan out," Roston said. "So in that particular industry, nano does not really bring positive connotations."

Small Gains

But InPore does provide a good case study in what happened to the nanotech companies that still exist in Michigan.

First, it uses a homegrown technology spun out in 1996 from the labs at MSU. Just a little over a year ago [in 2010], the company thought it had found a niche in making wind turbines. The material improved the strength of the epoxy used to hold the blade together.

It turned out, though, that while this was an improvement, it was a negligible one.

So InPore took the same material and decided to sell another characteristic: its ability to act with other materials as a flame retardant. There is a market demand, combined with a government regulatory push worldwide, for better flame-retardant materials in plastics because of concern over toxicity in the current technology.

Roston said InPore has signed nondisclosure agreements with 30 large companies, only two of them under $100 million a year in sales, which have been evaluating their materials. InPore now looks to raise $2 million, a portion of which will establish a pilot plant in the East Lansing area in the next year.

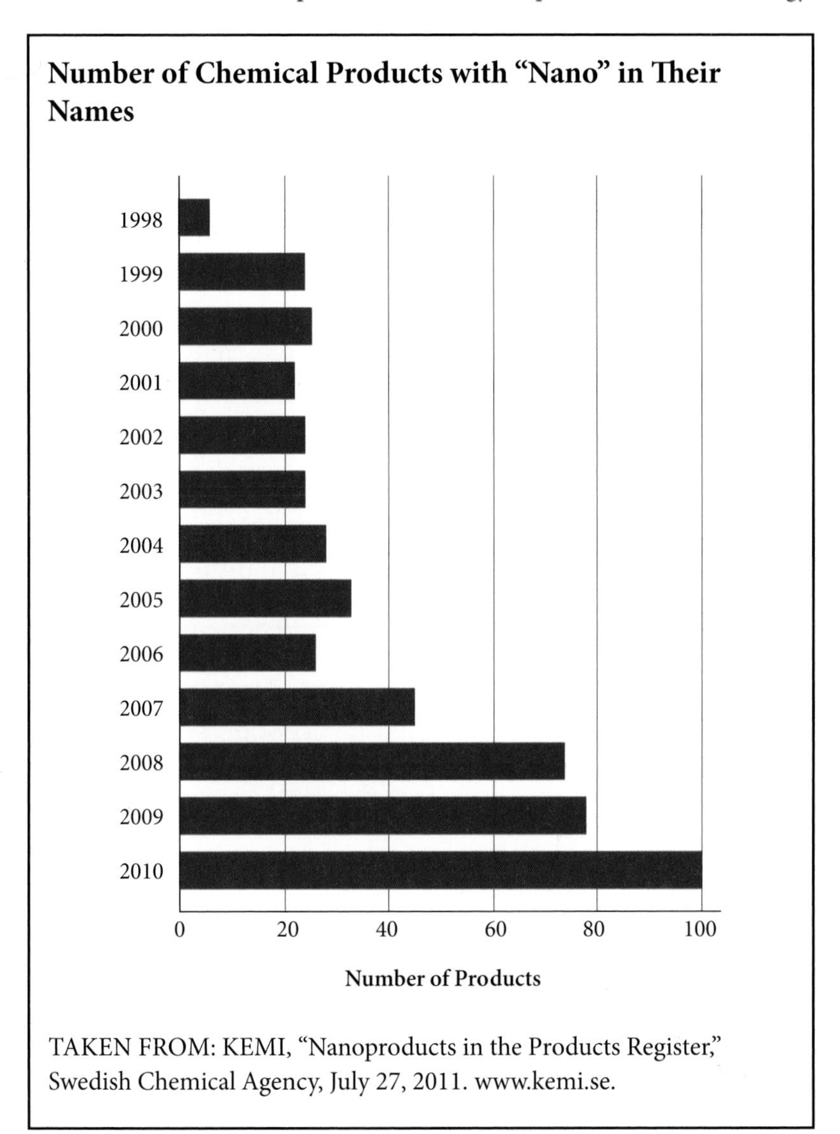

Number of Chemical Products with "Nano" in Their Names

TAKEN FROM: KEMI, "Nanoproducts in the Products Register," Swedish Chemical Agency, July 27, 2011. www.kemi.se.

InPore's technology is true nanotech because it is not simply about the size of the material but the way it's been engineered. The particles are porous—6-nanometer holes that are just the right size for a polymer to slip through and entangle itself with the fire-retardant nanomaterial, tying the strands together.

The result is a plastic that retains its flexible properties and can snap back into shape despite the addition of the nano additive.

No, this does not sound like the nanotech of science fiction. But it is the nanotech of today. And much of it has to do with the creativity of the entrepreneur rather than the quality of the invention itself. The business of nanotech is really about the entrepreneur's ability to find the right application, the right market at the right time. The scientists themselves often do not know how their breakthroughs actually will find markets.

That is why Michael Kelly was brought onboard as CEO and president of the Ann Arbor-based nanotech company Nanocerox—to bring the company out of its research mindset and start finding more commercial applications. Until now, Nanocerox has been living off U.S. Department of Defense grants for its materials to be incorporated into weapons systems that Kelly is not even allowed to disclose. And the defense business is fine, as far as it goes.

"It's a nice model to build upon, but not to rely on," Kelly said.

Nanocerox is expanding its Ann Arbor operations as it finds dual-use applications for its military technology. Anticounterfeiting is also a potential market.

"We have the ability with that technology to mark products that are only visible under certain wavelengths of laser," Kelly said. "So, we've basically added a fingerprint."

When Kelly came onboard six months ago, he said: "I shocked them a little bit. This is the real world now. You're actually getting this stuff ready for the commercial marketplace. Totally different from the military marketplace. It's totally different in execution, demands, needs, wants. And if you can survive that, you'll be a success."

Success

And success is what happened to one company that was able to focus and deliver for commercial customers. What began two decades ago as T/J Technologies, born from the strength of a nanophosphate breakthrough at the University of Michigan, is finally seeing the light of day inside new lithium-ion batteries in GM electric vehicles.

T/J Technologies, which was bought by Massachusetts-based A123 Systems Inc. in 2008, is another good case study that shows the real, albeit slow, pace of nanotechnology from lab to product.

Levi Thompson, a professor of chemical and mechanical engineering at UM, co-founded the company with his wife, Maria, about 20 years ago. Like many startups, it took a number of years to stabilize, Levi Thompson said. It was around 1995 that the company decided to focus on battery materials.

The eventual acquisition by A123 came about because T/J Technologies was looking for a way to get in on Michigan's push to make the state a center of battery manufacturing for electric vehicles.

"The state's investment in this area, in the lithium-ion battery area, was absolutely critical," Thompson said.

But so was the persistence of vision within the company. "Everything has to be tested by the market," Thompson said. "You have to take it out and see what the market says about it. You might think it's great, but if the market is not willing to accept it because of a combination of things—cost, performance, intellectual-property challenges—all of it wrapped up determines whether the market is interested."

Thompson is no longer with the company and is back in the lab working on the next nano thing. This time it's a new company, based in Plymouth, called Inmatech, which is working on a way to make high-energy-density batteries work better.

So, nanotech is, indeed, beginning to fulfill its promise of making products better. But it's not the get-rich-quick scheme that many envisioned a decade ago.

In the end, it's happening at the pace of any other technological development—a combination of the right technology at the right time in the right place and supported by people with vision. Michigan has companies and people that fit the bill. But, said Nanocerox's Kelly, it's a business just like any other in Michigan. And that means no matter how wonderful the technology, it takes focus to stay alive.

"If you're running a focused operation and if you know where your journey's going, I think you're in good shape," he said. "But it's still really rough in Michigan."

Viewpoint 3

> *"Nanotechnology was singled out as a target for [terrorist] attacks."*

Fear of Nanotechnology Has Resulted in Terrorist Violence

Marion Lloyd and Jeffrey R. Young

Marion Lloyd is an education researcher at the National Autonomous University of Mexico and a former correspondent for the Boston Globe *and other publications. Jeffrey R. Young is on the editorial staff of the* Chronicle of Higher Education. *In the following viewpoint, they report on a package bomb that injured nanotechnology researchers at the University of Mexico. Credit for the bomb was claimed by a group who said that they were opposed to nanotechnology research because it was dangerous to humanity. Lloyd and Young say that the dangers discussed by the bombers seem to be linked to science fiction scenarios and are wildly overblown. They relate the bombers to the Unabomber, who mailed package bombs to technology researchers and killed three people over the period from 1978 to 1995.*

As you read, consider the following questions:

1. Who was the Unabomber, as described by Lloyd and Young?

Marion Lloyd and Jeffrey R. Young, "Nanotechnologists Are Targets of Unabomber Copycat, Alarming Universities," *The Chronicle of Higher Education*, August 21, 2011.

2. What new security procedures do the authors say that the university added in the wake of the bombings?
3. What is ELF Switzerland, as described by Lloyd and Young?

A package bomb that injured two professors at a university here [in Mexico City] this month [August 2011] is the latest in a string of attacks by a new terror group inspired by the Unabomber. Its violent actions have put campuses across Mexico on alert and caused nanotechnology researchers worldwide to take precautions with their mail.

Heirs of the Unabomber

Nanotechnology was singled out as a target for the attacks in manifestos posted on the Web by the group behind the bombs, which calls itself "Individualities Tending Toward Savagery." It has been linked to attacks in France, Spain, and Chile, and to a bomb sent earlier this year to a scientist at another Mexican university who specializes in nanotech. An analyst who helped identify the Unabomber—who turned out to be a former professor—says the posts show signs of someone well-educated who could be affiliated with a college.

The online rants credit the Unabomber as an inspiration. The Unabomber, a former professor of mathematics at the University of California at Berkeley named Theodore Kaczynski, spread fear in academe for nearly 20 years with his mail-bombing campaign, which killed three professors and wounded 23 others until he was arrested, in 1996. Today he sits in a federal prison in Colorado with no chance of parole, but he continues to write articles calling for a revolution to achieve his dream of an end of technology and a return to hunter-gatherer societies.

The new group's latest package exploded in an office on the campus of the Monterrey Institute of Technology and Higher Education, outside of Mexico City, in early August.

The blast wounded its intended target, Armando Herrera Corral, director of a technology-transfer center, which the group's manifesto said is key to the university's plan to promote research projects that "are relevant for the progress of nanobio-industry within the country."

The explosion also wounded a nearby colleague, Alejandro Aceves López, director of the university's graduate school of engineering and science. Both men are expected to recover from their injuries.

Officials closed the campus for a day and have added new security procedures, which include the use of metal detectors at all campus entrances, random sweeps of campus areas with metal detectors, and searching the cars of some students, according to a statement.

The university also sent e-mails to parents of its students (in English translation to the parents of its approximately 100 foreign students) explaining the new security measures, according to a university public-relations official who asked not to be named, because he was not authorized to discuss the incident. The official said all of the foreign students decided to remain on campus.

Nanotechnologists as Targets

In the group's online post (written in Spanish) claiming credit for the latest bombing, the terrorists complained about the growing number of nanotechnology experts in Mexico, which it estimated at 650. "The ever more rapid acceleration of this technology will lead to the creation of nanocyborgs that can self-replicate automatically without the help of a human," it said.

Such a scenario was popularized in Michael Crichton's 2002 novel, *Prey* (though the post did not cite the work), in which microscopic robots escape from a lab and take over people's bodies. The manifesto argues that nanoscientists "have given their lives for years in the name of human self-destruction." Scientists say the notion is pure science fiction.

The same group sent a parcel bomb to a nanotechnology researcher at the Polytechnic University of the Valley of Mexico in April. That package was addressed to "Oscar Camacho" but apparently was intended for the head of the nanotech department, Carlos Alberto Camacho Olguín. The bomb detonated and wounded a security guard; the professor was unharmed.

In early May the group sent another bomb to the same university, but the package was intercepted, and no one was injured.

In an online manifesto published soon after those attacks, the group threatened more violence. "Last month we made an attempt against Oscar Camacho, today against the institution, tomorrow who knows?" it said. "Fire to the development of nanotechnology, together with those who support it."

Increased Security

Mexican law-enforcement officials have called on universities around the country to beef up their security.

The University of the Americas–Puebla, said to be the first institution in the country to set up a nanotechnology major, sent an e-mail message to all students, professors, and staff members alerting them not to open suspicious packages, and held a meeting to discuss other security measures.

"When I heard the news about what happened at Monterrey Tech, I was very worried, because of the large number of students that we have in the program here," says Miguel Ángel Méndez Rojas, coordinator of the university's nanotechnology program, in an e-mail message. "Because we were the first undergraduate program in Mexico, we felt we could be a target."

It was "devastating" to read the group's online manifestos, he says. "I'm convinced that the group's phobia of science (and nanotechnology and its risks) comes mostly from ignorance and misinformation."

Many people in the region are skeptical of science, he adds. "In our country, and in the whole Latin American region, we put more faith in the supernatural than in reason. This poses fatal consequences, making people view researchers in science and technology with suspicion and hate, as inhuman individuals, who work against society and as the exploiters and destroyers of natural resources."

Alfredo Castillo, attorney general in the State of Mexico, where Monterrey Tech is located, said in a news conference that the terrorist group has ties to acts of violence in other countries, although he did not provide details and did not respond to requests for an interview.

Last month members of a group called the ELF Switzerland Earth Liberation Front were sentenced to prison for plotting to bomb an IBM laboratory that does nanotechnology research in Switzerland. It is not clear whether that group has any ties to the Mexican terror group.

Watching Their Mailboxes

Though most nanotechnology researchers in the United States are not as nervous as their Mexican colleagues, some are watching the situation—and their mailboxes—closely.

"We've warned our faculty and staff and students to be wary of packages, but we're not too concerned at this moment," says Wade Adams, director of Rice University's Richard E. Smalley Institute for Nanoscale Science and Technology.

Some U.S. nanotechnology researchers have not yet heard of the bombings, though, or say they feel that risks to their own labs are minuscule.

Among the latter is Ian T. Ferguson, chairman of the department of electrical and computer engineering at the University of North Carolina at Charlotte, who works on nanotech projects. "Driving on the road is problematic," he says, putting the risk in perspective. "Today I was driving behind a truck and its tire blew out," which almost caused a crash. "Do I stop driving? No way."

Jack Levin, a professor of sociology and criminology at Northeastern University, says he is not surprised to see others follow the Unabomber's pattern of mail bombings followed by antitechnology screeds [essays]. "I don't think we should be surprised that killers are inspired by other killers," he says. For such criminals, the main goal of producing manifestos is to justify their violent actions and portray themselves as heroes rather than villains, he argues. "The terrorists are motivated as much from personal pathology as they are from politics or science or antiscience."

Some experts wonder whether the bombs in Mexico are the work of a group or the actions of a lone attacker presenting himself as a group in his writings.

"Much of it is written in the plural possessive pronoun 'we,' but there are occasions where the singular personal pronoun was used by the author," says Randall G. Rogan, a professor of communication at Wake Forest University. He is an expert on author identification and served on the team of analysts that helped identify the Unabomber, who signed his own manifesto as the work of a group, which he called the Freedom Club.

Based on initial readings of two of the manifestos, Mr. Rogan guesses that the writer has some sort of college education and could even be affiliated with a college. "The author is drawing on data and drawing on references and quoting a variety of scientists"—all of which suggests academic training, he says.

Mr. Méndez, at the University of the Americas, agrees. He notes that the manifestos are full of references to American texts and suggest that the author, or authors, have a solid command of English. They also know how to use computer networks and technology, and how to build and handle explosives.

Such skills suggest a key contradiction in the group's anti-technology position, says Mauricio Terrones, a leading Mexican researcher in nanotechnology, who has worked outside the country since 2010. "They don't want technology, but they use it to make bombs with gunpowder, a battery, et cetera, and they also use the Internet to make themselves known," wrote Mr. Terrones, who is now a professor of physics at Pennsylvania State University, in an e-mail interview with *The Chronicle* [*of Higher Education*]. "If it weren't for science and technological development, they could never have gone public."

In the "endnotes" to its May manifesto, the group anticipates such criticisms. But it denies that its use of the Internet undermines its antiscience stance.

"Only in this way can we disseminate our ideas," the manifesto says. "Are you really stupid enough to think that we who criticize the Techno-industrial System would carve this manifesto in stone?"

For now, the bomber or bombers who struck Mexican campuses remain at large, acting, as they put it, "without compassion and without mercy."

Viewpoint 4

> *"Despite emerging evidence of potential toxicity to human health and the environment from* some *forms of nanotechnology under* some *circumstances, not much popular alarm has arisen."*

Few People Fear the Risks of Nanotechnology

Susanna Priest

Susanna Priest is the author of Nanotechnology and the Public: Risk Perception and Risk Communication *and edits the magazine* Science Communication. *In the following viewpoint, she maintains that people seem largely unafraid of the risks of nanotechnology, especially in comparison with concerns about biotechnology and genetically modified foods. She suggests that people see manipulating biology as more wrong or more dangerous than manipulating ordinary materials. She concludes that scientists could do better about investigating and publicizing possible downsides of nanotechnology, although overall, the fact that there is no public panic on this issue is a good thing. The original article may be found at http://www.the-scientist.com/?articles.view/articleNo/31674/title/Opinion--No-Objections-to-Nano-/.*

Susanna Priest, "Opinion: No Objections to Nano?," *The Scientist*, February 3, 2012.

As you read, consider the following questions:

1. What was Magic Nano, and why does Priest suggest it may not be a good example of nanotechnology's dangers?
2. What is the precautionary principle, as described by the author?
3. What is an "attenuated risk", and why does Priest think nanotechnology may be one?

Some forms of biotechnology have become notoriously controversial. Genetic modification of crops, for example, altered the food supply in ways some consumers found troublesome, either because of anticipated consequences, a lack of tangible benefit, lack of opportunity to participate in the decisionmaking, or simply a sense of inherent "unnaturalness." Stem cell research has raised similar uneasiness, albeit for entirely different reasons, largely moral beliefs that equate it with the destruction of human embryos. So far, though, public perception of nanotechnology does not seem to be headed in the same direction. Sure, there are appeals for regulation and isolated protests, but it doesn't seem as though there is really as much in the way of concerted will behind them. While some might be waiting for the other shoe to drop—I've been told many times that public concerns about nano are bound to emerge "just as soon as people understand what this is all about"—events so far suggest it may be a long wait.

No Worries

Despite emerging evidence of potential toxicity to human health and the environment from *some* forms of nanotechnology under *some* circumstances, not much popular alarm has arisen. Great uncertainty remains over *which* products and under *what* circumstances we should be concerned, but of course this hasn't stopped public reaction in the past. Several potential "triggering events" of the sort we social scientists might have expected would unleash underlying fears have already happened. In 2006, reports emerged of serious respiratory problems among German consumers using a household cleaning product called "Magic Nano," and evidence published in 2009 indicated severe lung disease and even deaths among a small group of Chinese factory workers exposed to nanoparticles (and many other chemicals, as it turns out). In both cases, the link between nanotechnology and disease is far from clear. "Magic Nano" may not even have contained nanoparticles; the label was apparently chosen in an attempt to hype the product, much like the name "iPod nano." Clearly, the marketers involved believed the word "nano" is attractive to consumers, rather than a source of concern for them.

To me, as a social scientist who studies risk communication, perception and reality are indeed the same thing, and so the interesting question is why, when uncertainty about risks has certainly not stopped public opinion from turning sour in the past, should nano be getting the benefit of the doubt while so much of bio remains persistently controversial?

The answer may lie in the nature of our technoscientific culture. I recently published a multi-year panel study involving 76 citizens of South Carolina, representing various walks of life, which reinforced the notion that because most Americans like technology, they are generally willing to give nanotechnology a pass, at least for now, even though they don't know much about it. About two-thirds of the panel held positive views, and the negative minority seemed to draw on negative expectations about technology more generally, rather than specific views about nanotechnology. Panelists' views changed little over the 32 months of the study. The most common concerns, reasonably enough, centered on unexpected consequences and unanticipated side effects. Indeed, people seemed

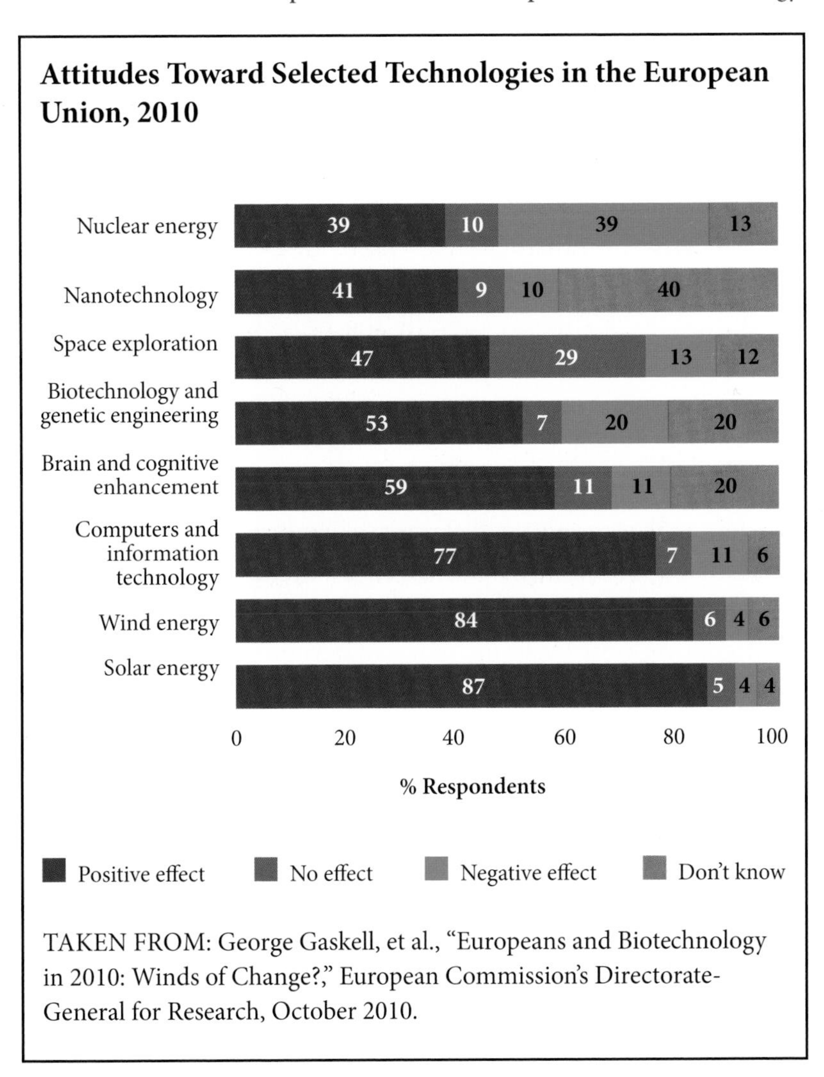

TAKEN FROM: George Gaskell, et al., "Europeans and Biotechnology in 2010: Winds of Change?," European Commission's Directorate-General for Research, October 2010.

perfectly aware of the uncertainties surrounding nano-associated risks, but this hardly appeared to induce fear.

To those of us who lived through the early years of the genetically modified (GM) food "wars," which some tended to attribute to a lack of familiarity alongside low levels of trust, this is pretty interesting. Nano involves many of the same sorts of key actors (major corporations, government regulators, scientists, engineers, and consumer advocacy groups) and, if anything, even greater levels of scientific uncertainty.

Yet there's something quite different about what we call the "climate of public opinion" for nanotechnology as opposed to biotechnology, particularly GM. To be sure, some observers are invoking the so-called precautionary principle (the largely European idea that we should not adopt a technology until the evidence shows it does not cause harm), but even in such cases it usually seems that they are calling for precaution because they think this is generally the right way to manage any new technology, rather than because nanotechnology is particularly worrisome.

Nano vs. Bio

So what makes nano so different from bio? Simply put, manipulating DNA simply seems to challenge our underlying cultural ideas about how the world ought to be in ways that manipulating otherwise ordinary materials does not.

For those who want to communicate about risk in a responsible way with the so-called "lay" or non-specialist public, nano represents a novel challenge. Rather than being an "amplified" risk, by which I mean one that the media and other social institutions have tended to highlight, nanotechnology may represent an "attenuated" risk, or one that these institutions have tended to ignore. If people are too fearful of a technology, they may lose out on its potential benefits, yet if too trusting, they may ignore important risks. But few among us really want to be the one yelling "Fire!" in a crowded world. After all, we're still not even sure there's a problem. Are we?

Indeed, just last month (January 25), the National Research Council issued a report calling for a coordinated research plan to investigate nanotechnology's poorly understood risks to both health and environment, lest its beneficial promise for society ultimately go unrealized.

Viewpoint 5

> "When people have an opinion (and an average of about half of those surveyed did not), they see more promise than peril in nanotechnology."

The US Public Knows Little About Nanotechnology but Mildly Supports It

John Besley

John Besley is an assistant professor at the School of Journalism and Mass Communications, University of South Carolina, Columbia. In the following viewpoint, he adduces research about public opinions of nanotechnology to argue that the media spend little time on nanotechnology issues and do little to shape public opinion on the issue. He adds that surveys show little public knowledge of nanotechnology, although it is perceived in a mildly positive light. He concludes that, while some have argued that public opinion of nanotechnology would improve with greater knowledge, there is little evidence from survey results that more knowledge is correlated with more approval.

As you read, consider the following questions:

1. What does most nanotechnology media coverage tend to focus on, according to Besley?

2. What percentage of people had heard nothing about nanotechnology in the yearly Woodrow Wilson Center polls, as reported by the author?
3. What does Besley say is the difficulty with rejecting the argument that knowledge is associated with attitudes?

As this article shows, a number of scholars in social science disciplines, such as political science and science communication, have turned their attention to exploring how individuals perceive nanotechnology's risks and benefits. Research in this area continues to provide a unique opportunity to track risk perceptions, whereas nanotechnology discussions are just beginning to appear in the public sphere. Many of those involved in this research, and cited below, had previously studied emerging technology areas, such as nuclear energy and agricultural biotechnology, and saw the opportunity to help decision makers avoid some of the communication missteps that proponents of previous technologies had committed. Technology advocates often point to these communication failures as the cause of unwarranted public health and environmental concerns. At the academic level, the emergence of nanotechnology as a potential subject of social research also corresponded with more general discussions within academia and government in both Europe and North America about the value of 'upstream' public involvement in science decision making. . . .

A Focus on Progress

In addition to the survey research described below, a number of systematic assessments of media content have also focused on nanotechnology, starting with a handful of studies in 2005. Building on similar work about previous emerging technologies, the nanotechnology content analyses show that most coverage tends to focus on technological process and, only rarely, health and environmental risks or ethical concerns.

Health and risk content appears to have become more common over time but, overall, coverage of any aspect of nanotechnology has continued to remain relatively rare. These initial content analyses looked at the United States, and the United Kingdom. More recent studies have looked in more detail at subissues such as nanoparticle safety, the emergence of more increased regulatory focus, economic coverage of nanotechnology, as well as coverage in smaller countries such as Denmark. Some recent studies have also relied on interviews with journalists who cover nanotechnology to emphasize the challenges of communicating uncertain science appropriately. Given the relative paucity of coverage, however, there is no evidence that the news media are driving the debate about nanotechnology.

Survey Findings

It is consistent with the low levels of media coverage and it should perhaps come as little surprise that the earliest and most consistent finding of nanotechnology survey research is that the public does not know much about nanotechnology. For example, one attempt . . . to synthesize the survey work up to 2008 shows that about half of respondents in the reported studies said they had no familiarity with nanotechnology. Annual telephone surveys conducted for the Woodrow Wilson Center starting in 2006, some of which were included in the summary study, report that in 2006 and 2007, 42% of respondents . . . said they had heard nothing about nanotechnology. This number rose to 49% in the 2008 survey and then backed down to 37% in 2009. At the same time, the number of people who said they heard 'a lot' about nanotechnology hovered between 24 and 31%. . . . Similar results from face-to-face surveys in the United Kingdom and telephone surveys in Canada and Japan were included in the summary study. An additional convenience sample study of (primarily) young people and more recent online studies from Germany and

France also found similar results in those countries. A broader European study, although not specifically asking about nanotechnology awareness, found that 53% of Europeans sampled in a 2004 survey said that they did not know enough to answer a question about whether nanotechnology 'will improve (their) way of life in the next 20 years (29%)' or whether it would have no effect (12%) or whether it will make things worse (6%).

One noteworthy aspect of the research underlying the consensus that the public know little about nanotechnology is that most of the data focus on respondents' self-reported level of awareness. Few studies include tests specifically meant to assess knowledge (that is, true/false tests). When administered, these tests indicate that, on balance, respondents generally understand that nanotechnology is an economic issue, is invisible to the naked eye and involves the modification of materials.

Benefits Outweigh Risks

Beyond reports of low knowledge levels, the second most common survey feature is the finding that when people have an opinion (and an average of about half of those surveyed did not), they see more promise than peril in nanotechnology. Most of this research involves asking survey participants directly whether they think nanotechnology will be, on balance, good or bad. For example, the Peter D. Hart Associates research for the Woodrow Wilson Center asks respondents to indicate whether 'benefits will outweigh the risks,' 'benefits will about equal the risks,' 'risk will outweigh the benefits' or whether the respondent is 'not sure'.

In contrast, telephone surveys . . . as well as mail surveys . . . ask multiple questions about specific potential risks of nanotechnology, followed by multiple questions about the potential benefits of nanotechnology. The goal in doing so was to ensure that the survey assessed the range of potential risks

Media Coverage of Nanotechnology

Since 1997, the emergence of neuroscience and nanotechnology news stories has . . . coincided with that of general nanotechnology and health nanotechnology coverage. Since the late 1990s, neuroscience has been interested in applying nanotechnology to health issues, particularly to healing brain and nerve diseases and improving brain function. These scientific developments might be enough to attract moderate attention from journalists. However, despite the continued growth of neuroscience nanotechnology research and development, there could be at least two possible explanations for the recent decline in press coverage. First, it is possible that the number of newsworthy events that would attract media attention, such as the Nobel Prize for the discovery of buckyballs in 1997, have been rare in recent years. Another possible explanation for the recent dip in neuroscience nanotechnology is the shifts underway within journalism. The number of science writers and reporters has declined in recent years, and mass media, including newspapers, are also assigning only a small percentage of their news hole to science and technology issues compared to other topics.

Doo-Hun Choi, Anthony Dudo, and Dietrem A. Scheufele, in Nanotechnology, the Brain, and the Future, *2013.*

and benefits. One mail survey-based study used a hybrid approach asking for a direct weighting of relative risks and benefits, as well as questions specifically about perceived health and environmental risks. Although the different approaches to measurement still point to more positive than negative attitudes about nanotechnology, risks and benefits may also interact to amplify or attenuate the impact of such perceptions on willingness to accept nanotechnology.

How Awareness Relates to Attitude

Beyond simply describing nanotechnology awareness and perceived risks and benefits, most academic studies of nanotechnology opinion attempt to test the degree to which specific factors are driving opinion. As might be expected, the most common relationship assessed is the one between awareness and perceived risks and benefits. This focus on the relationship between knowledge and attitudes toward science has been the subject of substantial research for many years. Although scientists often appear to believe that, if people just knew more, they would have more positive attitudes toward its products, academic research on this topic tends to show that that knowledge has relatively limited impact on attitudes toward emerging technologies. Science communication scholars have come to use the term 'deficit model' as a term-of-art in critiques of actors—usually scientists—who expect that increased scientific knowledge will inevitably lead to increased public acceptance of science.

The difficulty with critiquing the argument that knowledge is associated with attitudes is that the relationship sometimes exists. Indeed, a meta-analysis ... which focuses on similar themes to those described here ... confirms that the available nanotechnology data suggest that increased self-reported awareness is associated with marginally more positive views. Online surveys from Germany and France ... appear to suggest that awareness is associated with more positive views about nanotechnology after demographic controls and several additional explanatory variables. However, the studies that use the more elaborate test-based measures of knowledge (rather than self-reported awareness) find that basic science literacy rather than nanotechnology specific literacy is the more important predictor of positive views about nanotechnology, although it is impossible to compare these studies directly because the latter studies focus on dependent variables, such as support for nanotechnology policies, rather than risks and benefits. One mail survey-based study that uses both an awareness self-report and a short, general science literacy quiz finds that although awareness is associated with lower risk perceptions, general science knowledge is not. This study, however, uses only a limited regional sample.

"Religious respondents showed the highest level of opposition to . . . nanotechnology."

Religious Individuals Tend to Be Less Supportive of Nanotechnology

Dominique Brossard, Dietram A. Scheufele, Eunkyung Kim, and Bruce V. Lewenstein

Dominique Brossard is an assistant professor in the School of Journalism and Mass Communication at the University of Wisconsin–Madison (UWM); Dietram A. Scheufele is a professor in the Department of Life Sciences Communication at UWM; Eunkyung Kim is a doctoral student in the School of Journalism and Mass Communication at UWM, and Bruce V. Lewenstein is a professor of science communication at Cornell University. In the following viewpoint, they argue that attitudes toward nanotechnology are influenced by religious attitudes. Religious individuals tend to be more skeptical of nanotechnology. Knowledge of nanotechnology affects other attitudes as well, the authors maintain, but religious attitudes affect to what extent increased knowledge is linked to increased acceptance.

Dominique Brossard, Dietram A. Scheufele, Eunkyung Kim, and Bruce V. Lewenstein, "Religiosity as a Perceptual Filter: Examining Processes of Opinion Formation About Nanotechnology," *Public Understanding of Science*, vol. 18, no. 5, September 2009, pp. 546–558.

As you read, consider the following questions:

1. What concerns did the Church of Scotland representative have about possible applications of nanotechnology, according to the authors?
2. According to the authors, what do media stories about nanotechnology tend to focus on?
3. According to Brossard, Scheufele, Kim, and Lewenstein, how should science communication and outreach efforts change in light of their findings?

Using national survey data, we examine how people use science media, factual knowledge related to nanotechnology, and predispositions such as strength of religious beliefs, to form attitudes about nanotechnology. We show that strength of religious beliefs is negatively related to support for funding of the technology. Our findings also confirm that science media use plays an important role in shaping positive attitudes toward the technology. Overall public support for funding nanotechnology is not directly related to levels of knowledge among the electorate, but on risk and benefits perceptions and the use of media frames. However, knowledge about the technology does tend to be interpreted through the lens of religious beliefs and therefore indirectly affect levels of support.

A Fast-Growing Area of Research

Nanotechnology is one of the fastest-growing areas of research in the United States, with federal and private funding being funneled to universities for both basic and applied research. In his State of the Union speech on 31 January 2006, President [George W.] Bush proposed to double funding for emerging areas of research, including nanotechnology, over the course of the next 10 years. And consumers are already seeing over 500 commercial applications on the market. The American public, at least for now, seems to focus mostly on these novel applications and their potential benefits and is not particularly interested in or concerned about the potential risks of the new technology.

This phenomenon can at least in part be explained by the fact that most applications of nanotechnology so far have been in areas that are relatively uncontroversial, such as clothing or cosmetics. However, new sub-areas, such as nanobiotechnology or agrifood applications of nanotechnology will have an increasingly important impact on people's lives, and the question that needs to be asked is if these "nano-bio" applications will trigger public concerns that are similar to those that we saw for agricultural biotechnology, when they reach the marketplace.

Previous research on public perceptions of new technologies has largely focused on the potential incompatibilities between "knowledge deficit" models, on the one hand, and more emotional or predispositional variables on the other hand. Knowledge and understanding are, at best, very weak predictors of public support. Independently of its primary focus, however, most research in this area so far has paid little attention to the idea that *the context* in which people perceive a new technology and in which they interpret related knowledge facts is an important factor determining how individuals process information related to possible risks.

Specifically, we argue in this article that people use perceptual filters as interpretative frameworks to help them make sense of complex knowledge when reaching judgments about a controversial technology. More particularly and as we will discuss, we expect religiosity to be one of these perceptual filters in the case of nanotechnology. In order to complement recent research examining the formation of public attitudes toward nanotechnology, we also examine the potential role of mass media in attitude formation. Finally, we consider how public understanding of nanotechnology and perceptions of its related risks and benefits might impact attitudes, and place this discussion within the current broad debate around the ambiguous nature of "scientific literacy" in modern societies. Our examination of support for nanotechnology will focus more specifically on attitudes toward federal funding of nanotechnology since the issue of public support for expanded research and funding is increasingly important in order to sustain federal funding initiatives and maintain general support for science and technology in the political arena.

Religiosity and Nanotechnology

With science and religion providing a different understanding of the nature of the world, the interplay between religious beliefs and technological innovations has always been complex. Recent research has shown that religious beliefs can play an important role in shaping public attitudes toward science and technology. Given the normative inconsistencies between science and technology and religious belief systems, this finding is not very surprising. For instance, some people may feel that science interferes with nature or is equivalent with playing God and is therefore incompatible with strong religious beliefs. [Researchers George] Gaskell et al. found that moral issues and concerns about "unnatural" technologies were important in explaining negative attitudes toward genetically modified (GM) organisms. These technologies were seen as disturbing nature and natural processes, and perceived as risky and immoral. Respondents who held strong religious beliefs were more likely to show strong opposition to GM related scientific research that involved human beings.

The potential conflict between religiosity and science has also been discussed for nanotechnology. According to the official definition of nanotechnology as provided by the US Food and Drug Administration (FDA), "nanotechnology" is based on Nano-Bio-Info-Cogno (NBIC) technologies that emphasize the unity of nature at the nanoscale, as well as intelligible processes of evolution that have constructed life and intelligence, from the nanoscale, without divine intervention. This all-encompassing approach to nanotechnology, of course, may threaten many people's religious beliefs and make them more likely to oppose further research in that area.

While not necessarily rejecting technology per se, religious individuals might also be more cautious about its potential ethical implications and consequences for the human species. A writer in *Christianity Today*, a religious magazine, argues: "Christians must not become techno-dystopians, suspicious of all new technologies. While converging technology is not our salvation, neither is it intrinsically evil. Technology has enhanced our ability to show compassion and to spread the gospel". But some religious leaders have also expressed very concrete concerns over nanotechnology. For example, the head of the Church of Scotland's "Society, Religion and Technology Project" warns that use of nanotechnology might help create "a superhuman soldier" or "enhanced humans".

It is therefore reasonable to assume that nanotechnology will be perceived by some religious respondents as potentially "going too far" and as being in conflict with their strong moral and religious beliefs. We therefore expect individuals' strength of religious beliefs to be a powerful predispositional factor explaining opposition to nanotechnology. On the basis of this reasoning, we put forth the following hypothesis:

> *Hypothesis 1*: Strength of religious beliefs will be negatively related to support for nanotechnology.

The Role of Mass Media

Science media coverage (in terms of content and valence) has also been shown to play an important role in changing attitudes toward specific technologies and science in general. In fact, some researchers have argued that the nature of media coverage of these technologies serves as a simple decision rule for audiences when forming attitudes.

While the amount of media coverage devoted to nanotechnology is still minimal, its tone has been overwhelmingly positive, with print stories focusing on the progress and potential economic benefits that the technology could bring. Even when the stories were focused on potential risks of nanotechnology, these risks did not overshadow the positive aspects of nanotechnology in most of the articles. Not surprisingly, this dominance of positive coverage of nanotechnology has also helped promote positive attitudes among audiences. Science media use therefore is critical in explaining attitudes toward nanotechnology, and we put forth the following hypothesis:

> *Hypothesis 2*: Science media use is positively related to support for nanotechnology.

Knowledge and Perception of Risk

As we discussed earlier, religiosity and science media use are likely to be important predictors of support for nano funding. But where does people's understanding of nanotechnology, or nano literacy, fit in? We expect that levels of understanding of nanotechnology and perceptions of its potential risks and benefits might come into play differently. More importantly, we also expect that strength of religious beliefs might temper or attenuate some of these effects.

The role of "knowledge" or "public understanding of science" in explaining public attitudes toward science has generated debate and disagreement among scholars. At one end of the spectrum are the scholars who argue that scientific knowledge is socially constructed, a matter of frame of reference and hard to quantify. Attempts to link knowledge and attitudes, in their view, are therefore useless. At the other end of the spectrum, technocratic approaches to science believe in a purely "cognitive deficit" model and argue that the lack of knowledge and understanding among the general public also explains its lack of support. Recent research suggests that the answer lies somewhere in the middle. Although also claiming that knowledge and understanding are hard to measure, these authors believe that a basic understanding of scientific facts is necessary to a modern enlightened citizenry.

However, recent research suggests that other factors might be more important than knowledge and understanding when it comes to explaining public attitudes toward technological innovations. Among those factors are emotional reactions to science and technology (e.g., fears, skepticism about benefits from science and technology, perceptions of risks and so on) that might have direct effect on public attitudes toward controversial technologies such as nanotechnology. In addition, levels of trust in scientists, regulatory authorities and industry could outweigh the role attributed to scientific knowledge. In fact, people who lack scientific knowledge might use social trust as a standing decision rule in order to reduce the complexity of decision-making processes related to science.

Results regarding the relationship between scientific knowledge and attitudes toward science are therefore mixed. In some instances, higher levels of scientific literacy have been linked to more positive views of science. Others have argued that the relationship between factual technical knowledge and the perceived risk related to a technology is tentative at best, has a limited impact in promoting positive views of a technology, and plays no significant role in predicting support for nanotechnology.

Moreover, research suggests that the relationship between scientific knowledge and public attitudes toward science could be more complex than previously assumed and that other factors might mediate the knowledge-attitude link. For instance, [researchers P.T.] Jallinoja and [A.R.] Aro found that there was indeed an association between knowledge about genes and attitudes toward genetic testing; however, more scientific knowledge did not simply lead to unambiguous approval of genetic tests. Instead, several factors, such as an increase in people's ability to seek and understand information about genetics, mediated the association between knowledge and acceptance of genetic testing.

In this study, we are interested in exploring the relationship between basic understanding of nanotechnology and support for this technology. In line with previous research findings related to general public support for new technologies (such as agricultural biotechnology or stem cell research), we do not expect a significant direct effect of levels of scientific knowledge on support for nanotechnology. This null effect, of course, cannot be formally hypothesized.

As we have discussed earlier, however, science literacy may interact with personal predispositions to influence support for nanotechnology. In particular, highly religious individuals might be opposed to nanotechnology on the basis of moral considerations. These individuals are likely to use these moral considerations as perceptual lenses in order to make sense of what they know about science in general and nanotechnology in particular. However, given the limited number of studies on the combined effects of scientific knowledge and religiosity on nanotechnology, we do not formally hypothesize these effects but simply put forth the following research question.

> *Research Question 1*: Does the link between scientific knowledge and support for nanotech funding vary for respondents with different levels of religiosity? . . .

Media, Religion, and Knowledge

As public levels of concern and awareness increase and as the public engages more and more in decision-making about new technologies, it is increasingly important for public officials and other stakeholders to develop a better understanding of how public opinion is formed and of how citizens make sense of information about nanotechnology. This [study] used national survey data to assess the degree to which levels of religiosity, levels of science media use, factual knowledge related to the technology, and perceptions of its risks and benefits, help explain attitudes toward nanotechnology. As hypothesized, we found a direct and negative relationship between strength of religious beliefs and support for funding of the technology. Our findings also confirmed that science media use plays an important role in shaping positive attitudes toward a technology in its early stages of development. Until now, media have framed nanotechnology mostly in terms of economic benefits and scientific progress, and this kind of coverage has also shaped people's perceptions of nanotechnology. And since media are likely to be the primary source of information about nanotechnology and its risks and benefits, it is not surprising that media use has a positive effect on public perceptions, at this point, with respect to funding for nanotechnology.

Informing the ongoing academic and policy debates surrounding the cognitive deficit approach to public understanding of science, our study showed that factual knowledge about nanotechnology does play a role in shaping attitudes, although that role is not central. Most importantly, we provided initial evidence for the idea that religiosity serves as an interpretive tool for audiences when making sense of nanotechnology. As expected, levels of knowledge did interact with religiosity. Not surprisingly, highly religious respondents showed the highest level of opposition to federal funding for nanotechnology. But more importantly, the link between knowledge and support for federal funding was significantly weaker for highly religious respondents than it was for less religious respondents. Our data therefore suggest that factual knowledge can play a role in shaping attitudes, but that the effect differs depending on people's predispositions. And for highly religious respondents, their strong belief system can help suppress potentially positive effects of knowledge on support for nanotechnology. . . .

With these considerations in mind, our study offers a new and more complex look at public perceptions of emerging technologies. Our findings show that factual knowledge does have an important role to play, as traditional models of public understanding of science would suggest. However, this effect is primarily present for people that do not have strong value predispositions such as religiosity.

In terms of policy implications of our findings, of course, however, it is important to keep in mind that overall public support for nanotechnology will depend not on levels of factual knowledge among the electorate, but on more applied heuristics, such as risk and benefits perceptions or other media frames. And as our study showed, factual knowledge tends to be interpreted through the lens of religious beliefs and potentially other predispositional factors not examined here. Our data therefore clearly show that it is critical for policymakers and science communicators to understand the complex interplay of all of these factors when trying to understand public opinion formation about new technologies. Similarly, science communication and outreach efforts need to take these findings into account and replace one-size-fits-all modes of communication with tailored messaging for specific subgroups, based on their levels of information, risk and benefits perceptions, and belief systems.

Periodical and Internet Sources Bibliography

The following articles have been selected to supplement the diverse views presented in this chapter.

Diane Ackerman	"Opinion: Nanotechnology Shock Waves," *New York Times*, May 6, 2012.
Craig Cormick	"Why Do We Need to Know What the Public Thinks About Nanotechnology?," *Nanoethics*, August 2009.
Bruce Dorminey	"Nanotechnology's Revolutionary Next Phase," *Forbes*, February 26, 2013.
Rose Eveleth	"Trolls Are Ruining Science Journalism," *Smart News* (blog), *Smithsonian*, February 18, 2013. http://blogs.smithsonianmag.com.
Lawrence Gudza	"Successful Innovation Depends on Engaging the Grassroots," SciDev.net, May 2, 2012. www.scidev.net.
Clark A. Miller	"Nanotechnology for Human Enhancement: What Does the Public Think?," NISE Network blog, April 26, 2010. www.nisenet.org/blogs.
Nanotechnology Industries Association	"Public View of Nanotechnology," February 16, 2011. www.nanotechia.org.
Phys.org	"Public Attitudes to Nanotechnology: Lessons for Regulators," September 21, 2009. http://phys.org.
PRNewswire	"Technology Awareness May Be Low, but Opinions Are Strong," September 6, 2012. www.prnewswire.com.
Terre Satterfield et al.	"Anticipating the Perceived Risk of Nanotechnologies," *Nature Nanotechnology* no. 4, 2009.

CHAPTER 2

How Will Nanotechnology Affect Health?

Chapter Preface

When we think of health care innovation, we tend to think of new cures for deadly diseases, of vaccines, or of innovative treatments; however, disease detection can be as important as a disease's cure. And one of the most promising fields of nanotechnology is in ferreting out health dangers before they even affect the human body.

Scientists have developed a number of nanosensors that offer great promise for improving food safety. For example, scientists at Rice University and the Massachusetts Institute of Technology (MIT) have developed very thin, color-changing gels that can be used to detect whether food is still fresh or has spoiled. The gels are made of layers of nanoscale polymers that change color in the presence of environmental changes. If a gel is sealed inside a package, and the packaged food goes bad, inspectors could see the color change and would immediately know there was a problem. Scientists say that the gels are cheap to produce; they would then be a cheap, quick way to improve food safety and protect public health.

Another developing technology is an "electronic nose" which uses nanotechnology to detect pathogens and poisonous pesticides. According to a June 13, 2013, article at the Nanowerk website, the developers hope the sensor technology can be used to detect such things as gas leaks in industrial settings or chemical warfare attacks in military contexts, as well as being used for food safety.

A different application of nanotechnology may help to detect date rape drugs. A date rape drug is a chemical placed in an alcoholic drink in order to incapacitate the drinker for purposes of sexual assault. In the United States, there are two hundred thousand cases of individuals being dosed with date rape drugs each year. Using nanotechnology, Professor Fernando Patolski developed a chemical that can be dropped into a drink and that will turn the liquid cloudy or hazy if a date rape drug is present. According to Gail Weinreb in a July 3, 2013, article at Globes, an Israeli website, the creators of the product, Drink Sciences Ltd., plan to market the product to bars, which could provide it to patrons, and to young women, who could test their own drinks to ensure their safety.

The viewpoints in this chapter examine other medical and health applications of nanotechnology, as well as some of the health risks associated with such technology.

VIEWPOINT 1

"Researchers in South Africa are working on a way . . . [of] incorporating [TB] drugs into nanoparticles."

Nanotechnology Shows Promise for Delivering Medications More Effectively

Munyaradzi Makoni

Munyaradzi Makoni is a science writer based in Cape Town, South Africa. In the following viewpoint, he reports that nanotechnology is being used in his country to develop tuberculosis treatments. Traditional tuberculosis treatments require patients to take numerous drugs in a carefully timed sequence, which can be very difficult to do. Nanotechnology treatments would be able to time the absorption of drugs into the bloodstream with greater accuracy. This means that patients might be able to take a single pill once a week, rather than multiple pills every day. Though there are still questions about nanomedicine's risks and toxicity, Makoni says that South African scientists are hopeful that nanomedicine may have a significant impact on diseases like sleeping sickness and malaria as well.

Munyaradzi Makoni, "Case Study: South Africa Uses Nanotech Against TB," SciDev.Net, November 24, 2010. www.SciDev.Net. http://www.scidev.net/en/health/nanotechnology-for-health/features/case-study-south-africa-uses-nanotech-against-tb-1.html.

As you read, consider the following questions:

1. What evidence does Makoni provide to show that TB is a serious health issue in South Africa?
2. What diseases could be treated by nanodrugs tailored for delivery to the site of infected tissue, according to Makoni?
3. Why can the adverse effects of nanomaterials be unpredictable, in the author's opinion?

Treating tuberculosis (TB) in developing countries is a problem. Patients struggle to stick to the routine of taking daily tuberculosis medication for months on end—particularly when they must travel long distances for a nurse to ensure they take the drugs. This and the side effects mean many give up before completing the course.

Old Drugs Repackaged

Lack of adherence means the 50-year-old drug regimen is failing as multidrug-resistant strains emerge. Chances are remote that it will be replaced anytime soon with new antibiotics.

But the days of clockwatching for TB patients may soon be over. Researchers in South Africa are working on a way to deliver that half-century old treatment in a new guise—incorporating the drugs into nanoparticles so they are released slowly into a patient's bloodstream, raising the possibility that daily pills could be replaced with a single weekly dose.

Nanotechnology research is not cheap but researchers are hopeful that money spent on expensive research and development will be worthwhile when pitched against savings in treatment costs and substantial gains in health.

And those gains are there to be made. TB is one of the leading causes of adult death in South Africa with approximately 460,000 new TB cases in 2007, according to the WHO [World Health Organization]. South Africa is ranked fifth on the list of 22 high-burden TB countries in the world.

First-line treatment for TB consists of a pill of each of four antibiotics—isoniazid, rifampicin, pyrazinamide and ethambutol—taken every day.

South African scientists from the Council for Scientific and Industrial Research (CSIR) have incorporated these drugs into nanoparticles that are invisible to the human eye. White blood cells take up nanoparticles because they look like foreign objects and, effectively, transport them throughout the body while releasing their cargo, says Hulda Swai, senior scientist at CSIR's Centre for Polymer Technology. "These nanoparticles have superior properties for absorption in the small intestine to improve bioavailability and uptake into the circulation," says Swai.

The safety and uptake of the nanoparticles is being tested in TB-infected mice and the effectiveness of the nanodrug is being compared to conventional therapy to see whether a weekly nano dose is as effective as the standard daily treatment regime.

Human trials for the antibiotic called Rifanano are scheduled for 2012.

Affordability Rules

But the trials are not spared problems that affect clinical trials in many developing countries.

"Manpower and animal models are not always available, and where available, the expertise specific for nanomedicine is scarce," Swai told *SciDev.Net*.

But the potential advantages of the technology make its pursuit worthwhile. If TB treatment is reduced to a once-a-week dose, the overall costs, both of the drugs and of employing healthcare staff, could be significantly reduced.

"Given savings as a result of lower dose and higher efficacy, the consequence of targeted delivery—releasing drugs only after reaching the position required in the body—treatments might actually become cheaper," says Bernard Fourie, chief scientific officer of Medicine in Need, a non-profit research organisation with a base in South Africa that aims to develop treatments and vaccines suited to the developing world.

Nanodrugs tailored for delivery to the lungs or other sites of infected tissues have the potential to stop cancer cell growth, better protect against infection and more effectively attack and kill viruses and bacteria without affecting healthy cells around them.

"Remarkable benefits to healthcare" could be expected over the next decade with the development of drugs, vaccines and other pharmaceuticals that will specifically target diseased cells, Fourie says. But the major question is whether such new technologies would also benefit poor populations, such as those in Sub-Saharan Africa where TB, HIV/AIDS and malaria continue to affect millions.

But Fourie believes South Africa's pharmaceutical industry is capable of adopting nanotechnology, and that availability and access to such nanomedicines shouldn't be a problem.

Swai agrees, saying: "Only a small fraction of treatment costs is actually related to the drug itself. The nanodrugs are designed to make use of cost-effective materials that are easily accessible and relatively cheap to manufacture."

And because the technology is home grown it will be less expensive to manufacture nanodrugs than to buy imported mainstream drugs, adds Swai.

CSIR researchers are also working on nanoencapsulating antiretrovirals and antimalarials, as well as second-line TB drugs used for resistant cases where the first-line drugs don't work.

For instance, nanoencapsulation can involve coating the anti-malaria drug chloroquine with nanomaterials that include liposomes which can deliver the drug by penetrating cell membranes, making their action on diseased cells more targeted and efficient.

Cases of Tuberculosis Worldwide, 2010

World region	Number (thousands)	Percent of global total	Mortality per 100,000
South East Asia	2,993	34%	31.0
Africa	2,529	29%	74.0
Western Pacific	1,927	22%	17.0
Eastern Mediterranean	565	6%	21.0
Europe	445	5%	7.4
The Americas	352	4%	5.5
Global	8,811	100%	24.0

TAKEN FROM: World Health Sciences, "Tuberculosis World Wide Statistics," 2010. www.worldhealthsciences.com.

CSIR is collaborating on this research with the African Institute for Biomedical Research in Zimbabwe, and the Kenya Medical Research Institute as well as institutes on other continents including the University of Brasilia and Federal University of Rio Grande du Sul in Brazil; India's Post Graduate Medical Research Institute and Life Care; and the University of Buenos Aires in Argentina.

The Potential Risks

Many researchers warn that the growing number of developing countries interested in nanomedicine need to be aware of the potential risks associated with nanotechnology. Janice Limson, head of the Biotechnology Department at South Africa's Rhodes University, says: "The potential applications for nanomaterials are phenomenal, but researchers do agree that any developments in this regard must be partnered with research into understanding toxicity."

Materials have different properties at the nanoscale. For example, gold is nonreactive but at the nanoscale it becomes a catalyst for reactions.

While these properties are what make nanotechnologies so useful, they may also have unforeseen adverse effects. Globally, researchers are only just beginning to understand the toxicity of nanostructures and it is the subject of extensive work by a number of groups in South Africa.

Andre Nel, chief scientist of the division of nanomedicine at the University of California in Los Angeles' NanoSystems Institute, says that there is a lot of interest in assessing whether the 'nanocarriers' that transport drugs have "hazardous effects that are different and independent from the drugs being delivered".

The former Stellenbosch University student says that so far the only studies on the effects of nanotechnology in animals have focused on industrial nanomaterials rather than those used in nanomedicine. He adds that the same screening methods will be used to look at the safety of nanodrugs.

Though unaware of any specific regulations to monitor the risk of nanodrugs in South Africa, Nel says most countries would like to have specific independent evaluation criteria for nanotherapeutics. But no set of risk factors specifically for nanotherapeutics has been indentified yet.

"Most agencies worldwide are basing their assessments on traditional methods of drug safety assessment in which the nanomaterial is regarded as an integral component of the therapeutic substance as there has been no special risk that evolved as a result of nanodrugs," he says.

But these hurdles do not prevent research teams in South Africa from forging ahead. The new TB drug delivery method has been slated for availability in government clinics in 2016.

And Swai and her team are already planning for the future. "We hope to undertake the nanoencapsulation of traditional actives—ingredients granted authorisation used in treating other diseases of poverty around Africa such as sleeping sickness, ascariasis, leishmaniasis, chagas disease, onchocercariasis," she says.

VIEWPOINT 2

> "[Nano]therapies . . . rely on particles about the size of viruses to ferry potent drugs directly to tumor cells."

Nanotherapy May Help Treat Cancer

Carolyn Y. Johnson

Carolyn Y. Johnson writes about health issues for the Boston Globe. *In the following viewpoint, she reports that scientists are trying to use nanotechnology to deliver anticancer drugs more directly to cancerous cells. They hope this will reduce side effects, making it possible to use more powerful drugs to attack cancer cells. Scientists also hope that nanotechnology will allow the mixing of drugs that could not be used in combination before because of the severity of their side effects.*

As you read, consider the following questions:

1. According to Johnson, why are the two nanoparticle drugs being developed by Cerulean believed to be less toxic than conventional chemotherapy?

2. What are drug cocktails, and why is nanotechnology important for their development, in the author's opinion?

3. What is an antibody-drug conjugate, as described by Johnson?

Hoping to create more effective cancer medications with fewer side effects, two Cambridge [Massachusetts] start-up companies are beginning to test therapies that rely on particles about the size of viruses to ferry potent drugs directly to tumor cells.

Potent, but Safe

Cerulean Pharma Inc. has launched clinical trials of tiny Trojan horse[1] –like particles aimed at lung, ovarian, and kidney tumors, and BIND Biosciences Inc. is evaluating targeted, drug-laden nanoparticles in an early-stage study of patients with various advanced cancers.

The efforts are part of a broader movement in medicine, where drug development has been merging with engineering at the smallest scale to enable "nanomedicine" that can better target and deliver medications, or detect disease. The techniques hold particular promise for cancer, where therapies are sorely needed that can target cancer cells and spare normal ones. The National Cancer Institute funds about $130 million in nanotechnology research each year.

"There is growing interest in delivering drugs that are too toxic and failed in clinical trials, and packaging them in a nanoparticle," said Piotr Grodzinski, director of the National Cancer Institute office of cancer nanotechnology research. "You can . . . benefit from their potency, but enable safe delivery."

1. Trojan horse is a destructive substance which gains access or entrance to a system by disguising itself as desirable.

The two nanoparticle drugs being developed locally [in the Boston metropolitan area] are given intravenously, like conventional chemotherapy, but they are believed to be less toxic to normal cells and more effective against cancer because they are designed to aggregate and be released at tumor cells.

Cerulean, which uses a nanoparticle attached to an extremely toxic chemotherapy agent called camptothecin, announced last week [early July 2012] it had enrolled 150 patients in a randomized study of its drug in patients with nonsmall cell lung cancer, and expects data to be ready for analysis at the end of the year. The company has also recently treated its first kidney cancer patient with a combination of its experimental treatment and the drug Avastin. It expects this month to administer the drug to an ovarian cancer patient in a trial at Massachusetts General Hospital.

Cerulean says it has found in early trials that its method allows the delivery of a highly toxic drug without most of the side effects associated with standard treatment. That opens up the possibility of not only using a drug with severe side effects, but also allowing researchers to combine it with other drugs.

Better Targeting

"I think where this technology excites us the most is in terms of these combinations, which heretofore might not have been thought possible because of the cumulative toxicity," said Dr. Edward Garmey, chief medical officer of Cerulean. He said reducing the harmful side effects of medications would be essential if cancer care is to evolve—as many expect it will—into "cocktails," or combinations of drugs, intended to keep a chronic disease in check.

He said that the company, which has 32 employees and raised slightly more than $70 million during the last five years, is planning further trials in gastric cancer and small cell lung cancer. It is also doing preclinical research on a technique for delivering short segments of RNA directly to tumor cells, a therapy that can be used to turn off particular errant genes.

Meanwhile, in April, BIND Biosciences reported results in the journal *Science Translational Medicine* from an early trial in patients with advanced cancer. The company, using technology developed in the laboratory of bioengineer Robert Langer at the Massachusetts Institute of Technology, crafted a nanoparticle carrying the drug docetaxel, capable of homing in on cancer cells by identifying a landmark on the surface of a number of cancer cells and the blood vessels that feed tumors.

Such techniques are similar in their general concept to a class of drug that garnered widespread attention at the meeting of the American Society of Clinical Oncology last month. That type of drug, called an antibody-drug conjugate, consists of an antibody that binds to a cancer cell, linked to molecules of a specific drug.

But Scott Minick, chief executive of BIND Biosciences, said his company's approach will allow flexibility to deliver a wide array of drugs because the therapeutic nanoparticle can be engineered to carry thousands of molecules of a drug.

The company, which has 35 employees and has raised about $90 million, plans to launch a larger cancer trial later this year, although it has not disclosed a specific tumor type. But it also sees other potential applications for the technology, in treating inflammatory disease and pain.

Viewpoint 3

> *"[We now have] a promising lead for developing strategies to prevent lung damage caused by nanoparticles."*

Nanoparticles Can Cause Lung Damage, but Scientists Can Reduce Risk

Oxford University Press

Oxford University Press is the largest university press in the world. In the following viewpoint the press asserts that there are many exciting potential medical uses for nanoparticles, but there are also concerns that nanoparticles may damage the lungs. Researchers have discovered the mechanism whereby nanoparticles appear to destroy lung cells and have had some success in counteracting these effects in mice. The author concludes that researchers may be on the way to developing a way to counteract the dangerous effects of nanoparticles, making them safer for use in medicine.

As you read, consider the following questions:

1. What are PAMAMs, and how do they relate to damage caused by nanoparticles according to researchers cited by Oxford University Press?

Oxford University Press, "Health Risks of Nanotechnology: How Nanoparticles Can Cause Lung Damage, and How the Damage Can Be Blocked," *Science Daily*, Oxford University Press, June 11, 2009.

2. What does the author list as some of the potential uses of nanoparticles?
3. Why do the researchers say, according to the author, that they will not be able to use the same autophagy inhibitor in humans that they used in mice?

Scientists have identified for the first time a mechanism by which nanoparticles cause lung damage and have demonstrated that it can be combated by blocking the process involved, taking a step toward addressing the growing concerns over the safety of nanotechnology.

Nanotechnology, the science of the extremely tiny (one nanometre is one-billionth of a metre), is an important emerging industry with a projected annual market of around one trillion US dollars by 2015. It involves the control of atoms and molecules to create new materials with a variety of useful functions, including many that could be exceptionally beneficial in medicine. However, concerns are growing that it may have toxic effects, particularly damage to the lungs. Although nanoparticles have been linked to lung damage, it has not been clear how they cause it.

The Cause of Lung Damage

In a study published online June 11, 2009 in the newly launched *Journal of Molecular Cell Biology* Chinese researchers discovered that a class of nanoparticles being widely developed in medicine—polyamidoamine dendrimers (PAMAMs)—cause lung damage by triggering a type of programmed cell death known as autophagic cell death. They also showed that using an autophagy inhibitor prevented the cell death and counteracted nanoparticle-induced lung damage in mice.

"This provides us with a promising lead for developing strategies to prevent lung damage caused by nanoparticles. Nanomedicine holds extraordinary promise, particularly for diseases such as cancer and viral infections, but safety concerns have recently attracted great attention and with the technology evolving rapidly, we need to start finding ways now to protect workers and consumers from any toxic effects that might come with it," said the study's leader, Dr. Chengyu Jiang, a molecular biologist at the Chinese Academy of Medical Sciences in Beijing, China.

The first nanomaterial was developed by German scientists in 1984. Nanomaterials are now used in a variety of products, including sporting goods, cosmetics and electronics. The fact that unusual physical, chemical, and biological properties can emerge in materials at the nanoscale makes them particularly appealing for medicine. Scientists hope nanoparticles will be able to improve the effectiveness of drugs and gene therapy by carrying them to the right place in the body and by targeting specific tissues, regulating the release of drugs and reducing damage to healthy tissues. They also envision the possibility of implantable nano devices that would detect disease, treat it and report to the doctor automatically from inside the body. The US Food and Drug Administration has approved some first-generation nanodrugs. One example is Abraxane, a nanoformulation of the anti-cancer chemotherapy paclitaxel.

Counteracting Lung Damage

Lung damage is the chief human toxicity concern surrounding nanotechnology, with studies showing that most nanoparticles migrate to the lungs. However, there are also worries over the potential for damage to other organs.

In the study, the researchers first showed, through several independent experiments, that several types of PAMAMs killed human lung cells in the lab. They did not observe any evidence that the cells were dying by apoptosis, a common type of programmed cell death. However, they found that the particles triggered autophagic cell death through the Akt-TSC2-mTOR signalling pathway. Autophagy is a process that de-

Nanoparticles and the Lungs

Inhalation experiments on rats have become especially well known in which it was empirically demonstrated that carbon nanoparticles can cause considerable lung damage. Their toxic potential increases as particle size diminishes and as the relative surface area of the particle increases. At high concentrations, high mortality is the consequence. The cause however is obstruction of passages in the lungs due to the agglomeration of particles, not the toxicity of the particles themselves. These results do not necessarily indicate any potential consequences for humans since the rats were exposed to unrealistically high concentrations of nanoparticles in the air they breathed, which ultimately led to asphyxiation. The fear has also been frequently expressed that the small size of nanoparticles might enable them to cross the blood-brain barrier. What might ensue is completely unclear. . . .

Risks of Nanodust Remain Unquantified

For numerous reasons, there are still no epidemiological studies that quantify the risks posed by nanoparticle dust. First, there still are hardly any suitable measurement procedures. Second, nanoparticles themselves are substantially more diverse with regard to their chemical composition, size, and structure than, for example, the particles released by road traffic, which substantially impedes empirical studies. Third, synthetic nanoparticles have not been released so far in such large amounts that an epidemiological study would produce reliable results in the one or other direction. Yet the ethical question is precisely whether the attempt should not be made to avoid the situation that an epidemiological study might lead to a positive result. A condition for a positive epidemiological result is, after all, that there has already been damage to the health of a statistically significant number of people or that there has been a sufficient number of premature deaths.

Armin Grunwald, Responsible Nanobiotechnology: Philosophy and Ethics, *2012.*

grades damaged materials in a cell and plays a normal part in cell growth and renewal, but scientists have found that sometimes an overactivity of this destruction process leads to cell death.

The researchers also found that treating the cells with an autophagy inhibitor known as 3MA significantly inhibited the process, increasing the number of cells that survived exposure to the nanoparticles.

"Those results, taken together, showed that autophagy plays a critical role in the nanoparticle-induced cell death," said Dr. Jiang.

The scientists then tested their findings in mice. They found that introducing the toxic nanoparticles significantly increased lung inflammation and death rates in the mice, but injecting the mice with the autophagy inhibitor 3MA before introducing the nanoparticles significantly ameliorated the lung damage and improved survival rates.

"These experiments indicate that autophagy is indeed involved in lung damage caused by these nanoparticles and that inhibition of this process might have therapeutic effects," Dr. Jiang said. "We will likely need to look for additional new inhibitors to block lung damage as this particular compound is not stable in humans, but this gives us a promising lead for the first time."

"Our study has identified the principle for developing such compounds. The idea is that, to increase the safety of nanomedicine, compounds could be developed that could either be incorporated into the nano product to protect against lung damage, or patients could be given pills to counteract the effects," Dr. Jiang said, adding that the findings could also provide important insight into how nanoparticles cause other toxic effects.

It is not clear whether other types of nanoparticles would cause lung damage via the same mechanism, but some may,

Dr. Jiang said. The group's research also suggests that blocking autophagic cell death could perhaps be useful in combating other causes of lung damage.

VIEWPOINT 4

> *"For all [of nano]technology's promise and relentless progress, major questions remain about nanomaterials' effects on human health."*

Amid Nanotech's Dazzling Promise, Health Risks Grow

Andrew Schneider

Andrew Schneider is senior public health correspondent for AOL News. In the following viewpoint, he argues that scientists have found that many nanoparticles have dangerous side effects. Even substances that are safe at regular size can become health risks when reduced to nanosizes. However, he says, regulatory agencies and scientists tend to look at the positive scientific and economic benefits of nanotechnology and downplay the risks. He concludes that refusing to seriously consider nanotechnology's downside may result in public health risks.

As you read, consider the following questions:

1. What is nano-titanium dioxide found in, according to the author?

2. How can nanoparticles enter the body, according to Schneider?

3. What is the difference between the EPA approach to nanotechnology and the FDA approach, in Schneider's view?

For almost two years, molecular biologist Bénédicte Trouiller doused the drinking water of scores of lab mice with nano-titanium dioxide, the most common nanomaterial used in consumer products today.

She knew that earlier studies conducted in test tubes and petri dishes had shown the same particle could cause disease. But her tests at a lab at UCLA's School of Public Health were *in vivo*—conducted in living organisms—and thus regarded by some scientists as more relevant in assessing potential human harm.

Halfway through, Trouiller became alarmed: Consuming the nano-titanium dioxide was damaging or destroying the animals' DNA and chromosomes. The biological havoc continued as she repeated the studies again and again. It was a significant finding: The degrees of DNA damage and genetic instability that the 32-year-old investigator documented can be "linked to all the big killers of man, namely cancer, heart disease, neurological disease and aging," says Professor Robert Schiestl, a genetic toxicologist who ran the lab at UCLA's School of Public Health where Trouiller did her research.

Nano-titanium dioxide is so pervasive that the Environmental Working Group says it has calculated that close to 10,000 over-the-counter products use it in one form or another. Other public health specialists put the number even higher. It's "in everything from medicine capsules and nutritional supplements, to food icing and additives, to skin creams, oils and toothpaste," Schiestl says. He adds that at least 2 million pounds of nanosized titanium dioxide are produced and used in the U.S. each year.

What's more, the particles Trouiller gave the mice to drink are just one of an endless number of engineered, atom-size structures that have been or can be made. And a number of those nanomaterials have also been shown in published, peer-reviewed studies (more than 170 from the National Institute for Occupational Safety and Health [NIOSH] alone) to potentially cause harm as well. Researchers have found, for instance, that carbon nanotubes—widely used in many industrial applications—can penetrate the lungs more deeply than asbestos and appear to cause asbestos-like, often-fatal damage more rapidly. Other nanoparticles, especially those composed of metal-chemical combinations, can cause cancer and birth defects; lead to harmful buildups in the circulatory system; and damage the heart, liver and other organs of lab animals.

Yet despite those findings, most federal agencies are doing little to nothing to ensure public safety. Consumers have virtually no way of knowing whether the products they purchase contain nanomaterials, as under current U.S. laws it is completely up to manufacturers what to put on their labels. And hundreds of interviews conducted by AOL News' senior public health correspondent over the past 15 months make it clear that movement in the government's efforts to institute safety rules and regulations for use of nanomaterials is often as flat as the read-out on a snowman's heart monitor.

"How long should the public have to wait before the government takes protective action?" says Jaydee Hanson, senior policy analyst for the Center for Food Safety, "Must the bodies stack up first?"

Big Promise Comes with Potential Perils

"Nano" comes from the Greek word for dwarf, though that falls short of conveying the true scale of this new world: Draw a line 1 inch long, and 25 million nanoparticles can fit between its beginning and end.

Apart from the materials' size, everything about nanotechnology is huge. According to the federal government and investment analysts, more than 1,300 U.S. businesses and universities are involved in related research and development. The National Science Foundation says that $60 billion to $70 billion of nano-containing products are sold in this country annually, with the majority going to the energy and electronics industries.

Despite the speed bump of the recession, a global market for nano-containing products that stood at $254 billion in 2005 is projected to grow to $2.5 trillion over the next four years, says Michael Holman, research director of Boston-based Lux Research. Another projection, this one from National Science Foundation senior nanotechnology adviser Mihail Roco, says that nanotech will create at least 1 million jobs worldwide by 2015.

By deconstructing and then reassembling atoms into previously unknown material—the delicate process at the heart of nanotechnology—scientists have achieved medical advancements that even staunch critics admit are miraculous. Think of a medical smart bomb: payloads of cancer-fighting drugs loaded into nanoscale delivery systems and targeted against a specific tumor.

Carbon nanotubes, rod-shaped and rigid with a strength that surpasses steel at a mere fraction of the weight, were touted by commentators at the Vancouver Olympics as helmets, skis and bobsleds made from nanocomposites flashed by. Those innovations follow ultralight bicycles used in the Tour de France, longer-lasting tennis balls, and golf balls touted to fly straighter and roll farther.

Food scientists, meanwhile, are almost gleeful over the ability to create nanostructures that can enhance food's flavor, shelf life and appearance—and to one day potentially use the engineered particles to craft food without ever involving a farm or ranch.

Yet for all the technology's promise and relentless progress, major questions remain about nanomaterials' effects on human health. A bumper sticker spotted near the sprawling Food and Drug Administration [FDA] complex in Rockville, Md., puts it well: "Nanotech—wondrous, horrendous, and unknown."

Adds Jim Alwood, nanotechnology coordinator in the Environmental Protection Agency's [EPA'] Office of Pollution Prevention and Toxics: "There is so much uncertainty about the questions of safety. We can't tell you how safe or unsafe nanomaterials are. There is just too much that we don't yet know."

What is known is by turns fascinating and sobering.

Nanoparticles can heal, but they can also kill. Thanks to their size, researchers have found, they can enter the body by almost every pathway. They can be inhaled, ingested, absorbed through skin and eyes. They can invade the brain through the olfactory nerves in the nose.

After penetrating the body, nanoparticles can enter cells, move from organ to organ and even cross the protective blood-brain barrier. They can also get into the bloodstream, bone marrow, nerves, ovaries, muscles and lymph nodes.

The toxicity of a specific nanoparticle depends, in part, on its shape and chemical composition. Many are shaped roughly like a soccer ball, with multiple panels that can increase reactivity, thus exacerbating their potential hazards.

Some nanoparticles can cause a condition called oxidative stress, which can inflame and eventually kill cells. A potential blessing in controlled clinical applications, this ability also carries potentially disastrous consequences.

"Scientists have engineered nanoparticles to target some types of cancer cells, and this is truly wonderful," says Dr. Michael Harbut, director of the Environmental Cancer Initiative at Michigan's Karmanos Cancer Institute. "But until we have sufficient knowledge of, and experience with, this 21st-century version of the surgical scalpel, we run a very real risk of simultaneously destroying healthy cells."

When incorporated into food products, nanomaterials raise other troubling vagaries. In a report issued in January [2010], the science committee of the British House of Lords, following a lengthy review, concluded that there was too little research looking at the toxicological impact of eating nanomaterials. The committee recommended that such "products will simply be denied regulatory approval until further information is available," and also raised the concern that while the amount of nanomaterial in food may be small, the particles can accumulate from repeated consumption.

"It is chronic exposure to nanomaterials that is arguably more relevant to food science applications," says Bernadene Magnuson, a food scientist and toxicologist with Cantox Health Sciences International. "Prolonged exposure studies must be conducted."

Given the potential hazards, public health advocates are calling for greater restraint on the part of those rushing nanoproducts to market. "The danger is there today in the hundreds of nano-containing consumer products being sold," says Jennifer Sass, senior scientist and nano expert for the nonpartisan Natural Resources Defense Council. "Things that are in the nanoscale that are intentionally designed to be put into consumer products should be instantly required to be tested, and until proper risk assessments are done, they shouldn't be allowed to be sold."

David Hobson, chief scientific officer for international risk assessment firm nanoTox, adds that the questions raised by the growing body of research "are significant enough that we should begin to be concerned. We should not wait until we see visible health effects in humans before we take steps to protect ourselves or to redesign these particles so that they're safer."

Size Comparison of Different Objects and Substances in Nanometers

Substance	Nanometers
Typeset period (.)	1,000,000
Cancer cell	10,000–20,000
Bacterium	1,000
Virus	100
Human antibody	10
Glucose molecule	1
Water molecule	0.1

TAKEN FROM: "Understanding Nanotechnology," National Cancer Institute Alliance for Nanotechnology in Cancer. http://nano.cancer.gov.

Hobson says that when he talks to university and industry nano scientists, he sometimes feels as if he's talking with Marie Curie when she first was playing around with radium.

"It's an exciting advancement they're working with," he says. "But no one even thinks that it could be harmful."

More on Why Size Matters

At a weeklong Knight Foundation Science Workshop on nanotechnology at the Massachusetts Institute of Technology in June [2009], five professors—four from the Cambridge school [MIT] and one from Cornell University—dazzled their fellow participants with extensive show-and-tells on the amazing innovations coming out of their labs.

At one point, one played a video of a mouse with a severed spine dragging his lifeless rear legs around his cage. A scaffolding made of nanomaterial was later implanted across the mouse's injury. Further footage showed the same rodent, 100 days later, racing around his enclosure, all four legs churning like mad.

When the five nanotech pioneers were asked about hazards from the particles they were creating, only one said she was watching new health studies closely. The others said size had no impact on risk: No problems were expected, since the same chemicals they had nano-ized had been used safely for years.

It's an argument echoed by researchers and nano-manufacturers around the globe. But those assumptions are challenged by the many research efforts presenting strong evidence to the contrary, among them Trouiller's study, which was published in November [2009].

"The difference in size is vital to understanding the risk from the same chemical," says Schiestl, who was a co-author on the UCLA study. "Titanium dioxide is chemically inert and has been safely used in the body for decades for joint replacements and other surgical applications. But when the very same chemical is nanosized, it can cause illness and lead to death."

Regulators Take a 'Wait-and-See' Approach

Many public health groups and environmental activists fear the government's lethargy on nanotechnology will be a repeat of earlier regulatory snafus where deadly errors were made in assessing the risk of new substances. "The unsettling track record of other technological breakthroughs—like asbestos, DDT, PCBs and radiation—should give regulators pause as they consider the growing commercial presence of nanotech products," says Patty Lovera, assistant director of Food & Water Watch. "This wait-and-see approach puts consumers and the environment at risk."

While the agency has many critics, the EPA, for its part, is pursuing an aggressive strategy on nanotechnology. Among nano-titanium dioxide's other uses, the particle is deployed as an agent for removing arsenic from drinking water, and last year [2009], the EPA handed out 500-page books of health studies on the particles to a panel of scientists asked to advise the agency on the possible risk of that practice. (Another EPA science advisory board held hearings into the hazards from nanosilver used in hundreds of products, from pants, socks and underwear to teething rings.)

The Food and Drug Administration's handling of nano-titanium dioxide provides a more emblematic example of the government's overall approach. Public health advocates and some of the FDA's own risk assessors are frustrated by what they perceive as the agency's "don't look, don't tell" philosophy. The FDA doesn't even make a pretense of evaluating nanoparticles in the thousands of cosmetics, facial products or food supplements that have already flooded the market, even those that boast the presence of engineered particles. Nano Gold Energizing Cream ($420 a jar) and Cyclic nano-cleanser ($80 a bar) are among the many similar products unevaluated by the agency.

Dr. Jesse Goodman, the FDA's chief scientist and deputy commissioner for science and public health, says the exclusion of cosmetics and nutritional supplements from its regulations is what Congress wants. Goodman adds that "there is a most definite requirement that manufacturers ensure that the products be safe" but says that compliance is essentially voluntary, with the FDA taking action only after an unsafe product is reported.

AOL News repeatedly asked what steps the FDA was taking regarding nano-titanium dioxide, whose risks are acknowledged by other regulatory bodies, including the EPA and the NIOSH. The slow-to-arrive answer from spokeswoman Rita Chappelle: "If information were to indicate that additional safety evaluation or other regulatory action is warranted, we would work with all parties to take the steps appropriate to ensure the safety of marketed products."

Chappelle says FDA scientists are conducting research that focuses on nano-titanium dioxide, but declines to offer any details. Several of the agency's own safety experts say they specifically have urged that the engineered structures not be used in any products they do regulate without appropriate safety testing.

Why Nano-Optimists Hold the Upper Hand

Many government investigators join civilian public health specialists in denouncing the scant money that goes to exploring nanomaterials' possibly wicked side effects. The 2011 federal budget proposes spending $1.8 billion on nanotechnology, but just $117 million, or 6.6 percent, of that total was earmarked for the study of safety issues.

The [Barack] Obama administration says it is being appropriately vigilant about nanotech. "This administration takes nanotechnology-related environment, health and safety very seriously. It is a significant priority," says Travis Earles, assistant director for nanotechnology in the White House Office of Science and Technology Policy. After taking office, he adds, "We were able to immediately increase the spending in those areas."

But Earles, in what has become standard federal practice, is more fixated on nanotech's upsides. "We are talking about new jobs, new markets, economic and societal benefits so broad they stretch the imagination," he says. Yes, "absolutely," there are reasons for caution, he says. "But you can't refer to nanotechnology as a monolithic entity. Risk assessment depends fundamentally on context—it depends on the specific application and the specific material."

There's some scientific basis for this emphasize-the-positive position. "Every time you find a hazardous response in a test tube, that should not necessarily be construed as a guarantee of a real-life adverse outcome," notes Dr. Andre Nel, chief of the division of nanomedicine at the California Nanosystems Institute at UCLA.

But there are two ways to proceed in the face of such uncertainty. One is to forge ahead, assuming the best—that this will be one of those times where the lab results don't correlate to real-world experiences. Another is to hit pause and do the additional testing necessary to be sure that sickened lab animals do not portend human harm.

For advocates of more precautions for nanotech, the latter is the only responsible course.

"From cosmetics to cookware to food, nanoparticles are making their way into every facet of consumer life with little to no oversight from government regulators," says Lovera from Food & Water Watch. "There are too many unanswered questions, and common-sense demands that these products be kept off the market until their safety is assured."

With a moratorium not a realistic option, the U.S. government, along with its counterparts abroad, is left to tread gingerly in responding to the emerging evidence of nanotechnology's potential hazards.

"They don't want to cause either a collapse in the industry or generate any kind of public backlash of any sort," says Pat Mooney, executive director of ETC Group, an international safety and environmental watchdog. "So they're in the background talking about how they're going to tweak regulations—where in fact a lot more than tweaking is required.

"They've got literally thousands of [nano] products in the marketplace, and they don't have any safety regulations in place," Mooney continues. "These are things that we're rubbing in our skin, spraying in our fields, eating and wearing. And that's a mistake, and they're trying to figure out what to do about it all."

Periodical and Internet Sources Bibliography

The following articles have been selected to supplement the diverse views presented in this chapter.

Maria Chiara Bonazzi Aspden	"Nanotechnology and the Fight Against Cancer," *The Guardian* (Manchester, UK), January 31, 2012.
Centers for Disease Control and Prevention	"Nanotechnology," January 12, 2012. www.cdc.gov.
Larry Greenemeier	"Nanoparticles Enlisted to Impede Alzheimer's-Inducing Brain Plaque," *Scientific American*, September 24, 2012.
Kate Johnson	"Detecting Lung Cancer with Nanotechnology," Medscape Today, September 18, 2012. www.medscape.com.
Kate Kelland	"Gold Nanotech Breath Test May Show Cancer Early," Reuters, August 30, 2009. www.reuters.com.
David Levin	"The Dangers of Nanotech," *Nova*, January 13, 2011. www.pbs.org.
Nano.org	"Groundbreaking Research Links Sunscreen and Alzheimer's Disease," August 24, 2009. www.nano.org.uk.
Nanotechnology Industries Association	"The Use of Nanotechnology in the Fight Against Tuberculosis," January 10, 2011. www.nanotechia.org
NineNews	"Sunscreen Found to Have Toxic Ingredients," March 5, 2013. http://news.ninemsn.com.au.
Scott E. Rickert	"Nanotechnology's 4,500-Year Health Record," Industry Week, February 20, 2013. http://www.industryweek.com.

Chapter 3

How Will Nanotechnology Affect the Environment?

Chapter Preface

One area where nanotechnology could have major environmental effects is on the development and delivery of pesticides—chemicals used to control insects or other creatures that destroy crops. This application of nanotechnology is still in its infancy, so the exact benefits and dangers are still unknown. Still, research in this area has begun, and scientists have started to look into the potential repercussions, both pro and con.

Scientists hope that nanotechnology could help to better regulate and target the delivery of pesticides. Pesticides are dangerous chemicals; if smaller amounts could be delivered effectively to plants, it could reduce environmental damage and health risks, both to the public and to agricultural workers. As Will Souter says in a December 7, 2012, article at Azonano.com, nanotechnology could "allow the use of pesticides with the absolute minimum risk of environmental damage." In addition, nanotech sensors could provide early warnings of whether pesticides are damaging plants or whether too much pesticide is getting out into the environment.

There are also potential risks with using nanotechnology for pesticides, however. Oregon State University (OSU) has been researching nanomaterials, and while the vast majority are not dangerous to humans, there are some that are. David Stone, an assistant professor at OSU who was interviewed by the website Nano, says that it is vital to test nanoparticles in real-world situations, since laboratory experiments do not always give an accurate picture of potential dangers.

The OSU scientists say that it is important for manufacturers to disclose whether they are using nanomaterials in pesticides. This is a serious issue, since it is not always clear when pesticides contain nanomaterials. William Jordan, a senior policy adviser to the Office of Pesticide Programs (OPP) at the US Environmental Protection Agency notes in an April 29, 2010, presentation that one pesticide on the market already contains nanoscale silver and that the pesticide was approved without the disclosure that it contained a nanomaterial. Jordan says that the OPP is working to identify pesticides that contain nanomaterials and making sure that the products comply with safety regulations. As nanomaterial pesticide research progresses, such safety precautions will become more and more important.

The viewpoints in this chapter look at other potential environmental benefits and dangers of nanotechnology.

Viewpoint 1

> *"So far the questions about whether nanoparticles are an environmental risk outnumber the answers."*

Nanotechnology May Present Dangerous Environmental Risks

Heather Millar

Heather Millar's writing has appeared in the Atlantic Monthly, Smithsonian, New York Times, *and numerous other publications. In the following viewpoint, she argues that nanoparticles are being used in a large number of commercial applications but that there has so far been little research on their possible health and environmental effects. Nanoparticles, she says, are difficult to study, and they have so many exciting applications that scientists tend to want to focus on those rather than on risks. However, she warns, environmental research on nanoparticles is vital if we want to avoid environmental health disasters like those that resulted from widespread use of such so-called miracle products as DDT and asbestos.*

As you read, consider the following questions:

1. According to Millar, what are some ways to make nanoparticles?

Heather Millar, "Pandora's Boxes," *Orion Magazine*, January/February 2013.

2. When did scientists first realize that nanomaterials exhibit novel properties, according to the author?
3. Why is it so difficult to answer a multitude of questions about nanoparticles, in Millar's opinion?

A pair of scientists, sporting white clean-suits complete with helmets and face masks, approach a prefab agricultural greenhouse in a clearing at Duke University's Research Forest. Inside are two long rows of wooden boxes the size of large horse troughs, which hold samples of the natural world that surrounds them—the pine groves and rhododendron thickets of North Carolina's piedmont, which at this moment are alive with bird song.

Big Unknowns

Looking a lot like the government bad guys in [the 1982 movie] *E.T.*, the two men cautiously hover over a row of boxes containing native sedges, water grasses, and Zebra fish to spray a fine mist of silver nanoparticles over them. Their goal: to investigate how the world inside the boxes is altered by these essentially invisible and notoriously unpredictable particles.

The researchers are part of a multidisciplinary coalition of scientists from Duke, Stanford, Carnegie Mellon, Howard, Virginia Tech, and the University of Kentucky, headquartered at Duke's Center for the Environmental Implications of NanoTechnology (CEINT), that represents one of the most comprehensive efforts yet to measure how nanoparticles affect ecosystems and biological systems.

So far the questions about whether nanoparticles are an environmental risk outnumber the answers, which is why the Duke scientists take the precaution of wearing clean-suits while dosing the boxes—no one's sure what exposure to a high concentration of nanoparticles might do. Among the few things we *do* know about them are that they sail past the blood-brain barrier and can harm the nervous systems of some animals.

The regulation of nanoparticles has been recommended for more than a decade, but there's no agreement on exactly how to do it. Meanwhile, the lid has already been lifted on nanotechnology. The use of man-made nanoparticles has spread into almost every area of our lives: food, clothing, medicine, shampoo, toothpaste, sunscreen, and thousands of other products.

Regulatory structures, both here and abroad, are completely unprepared for this onslaught of nanoproducts, because nanoparticles don't fit into traditional regulatory categories. Additionally, companies often shield details about them by labeling them "proprietary"; they're difficult to detect; we don't have protocols for judging their effects; and we haven't even developed the right tools for tracking them. If nanotechnology and its uses represent a frontier of sorts, it's not simply the Wild West—it's the Chaotic, Undiscovered, Uncontrollable West.

And yet, when I visit the boxes on a warm spring day filled with the buzzing of dragonflies and the plaintive call of mourning doves, they look perfectly benign and could easily be mistaken for a container garden. But there are hints that more is going on: each "mesocosm" (a middle ground between microcosm and macrocosm) is studded with probes and sensors that continually transmit data to CEINT's central computer.

As I instinctively squint my eyes to try and locate evidence of the silver nanoparticles inside each box, I realize I might as well be staring down at these research gardens from another arm of the galaxy. The scale of these two worlds is so disparate that my senses are destined to fail me.

Unpredictable Nanos

As with many things that are invisible and difficult to understand—think subatomic particles such as the Higgs boson, muons, gluons, or quarks—any discussion of nanoparticles quickly shifts into the realm of metaphor and analogy. People working in nanoscience seem to try to outdo each other with folksy explanations: Looking for a nanoparticle is like looking for a needle in the Grand Canyon when the canyon is filled with straw. If a nanoparticle were the size of a football, an actual football would be the size of New Zealand. A million nanoparticles could squeeze onto the period at the end of this sentence.

But what is a nanoparticle? The very simplest explanation is that a nanoparticle is a very small object. It can consist of any bit of matter—carbon, silver, gold, titanium dioxide, pretty much anything you can imagine—that exists on the scale of nanometers. One nanometer equals one-billionth of a meter. A nanoparticle may range in size from one nanometer to one hundred nanometers, although the upper boundary remains a matter of debate among scientists.

Nanoparticles exist in nature, but they can also be manufactured. One way is top-down: grinding up things that are big until they are really, really small, an approach used in nanolithography for electronics. Or you can make them from the bottom up, following instructions that read like a chemistry textbook: mixing one chemical with another by pyrolysis (heating a material in a partial vacuum), or with electrolysis (running a current through a liquid), or by other means.

But what do they look like? Raju Badireddy, a postdoctoral researcher, is happy to satisfy my curiosity. He greets me with a smile at the door to one of CEINT's basement labs and guides me around his little domain. For much of his work, Badireddy uses a "dark field" microscope that excludes certain wavelengths of light, reducing the "noise" in the image to provide unparalleled clarity. Sensing my anticipation, he doses a slide with silver nanoparticles similar to those in the mesocosm boxes in the forest, and slips it under the lens.

As I look into the scope, it fairly takes my breath away. There are so many dots of light that I'm reminded of staring up at the Milky Way on a trip across the Tibetan Plateau years ago. Yet the silver dots throb and undulate as if alive. Here and there, giant spheres of dust, as large as Goodyear blimps, porpoise through the nanoparticles. I pull back from the oculars, feeling as if I've intruded upon something private. This world is so close—it's even inside me—yet it looks so other, so mysterious.

Scientists don't really have a full theoretical foundation to explain reality at this scale. But all agree that one of the most important aspects of nanoparticles is that they are all surface. Consider a conventional chemical process: When one element is reacting with another, it's really just the surface molecules that are involved in the lock-and-key dance of classical chemistry. The vast majority of the molecules remain interior, and stable. But there are many fewer molecules in a nanoparticle, so most of the molecules are on the outside, thus rendering nanoparticles more reactive.

Myriad surface imperfections cause randomness to dominate the nano world. If you hit a billiard ball with a clean shot at the macro level, you can have a good idea where it will go. But at the nano level, a billiard ball might shoot straight up, or even reverse direction. These bits of matter are hot to trot: ready to react, to bond, and to do so in unpredictable ways.

This makes life at the nano scale more chaotic. For instance, aluminum is used everywhere to make soda cans. But in nanopowder form, aluminum explodes violently when it comes in contact with air. At the macro level, gold is famously nonreactive. At the nano level, gold goes the opposite way, becoming extremely reactive. Bulk carbon is soft. But at the nano level, if you superheat it, the molecules bend into a tube that is very strong and semiconductive. In the nano world, gravity fades to the background, becoming less pronounced, the melting temperature of materials changes, and colors shift. At 25 nanometers, spherical gold nanoparticles are red; at 50 nanometers they are green; and at 100 nanometers they're orange. Similarly, silver is blue at 40 nanometers and yellow at 100 nanometers.

So chemistry and physics work differently if you're a nanoparticle. You're not as small as an atom or a molecule, but you're also not even as big as a cell, so you're definitely not of the macro world either. You exist in an undiscovered country somewhere between the molecular and the macroscopic. Here, the laws of the very small (quantum mechanics) merge quirkily with the laws of the very large (classical physics). Some say nanomaterials bring a third dimension to chemistry's periodic table, because at the nano scale, long-established rules and groupings don't necessarily hold up.

These peculiarities are the reason that nanoparticles have seeped into so many commercial products. Researchers can take advantage of these different rules, adding nanoparticles to manufactured goods to give them desired qualities.

Novel Properties

Scientists first realized that nanomaterials exhibit novel properties in 1985, when researchers at Rice University in Houston fabricated a Buckminsterfullerene, so named because the arrangement of sixty carbon atoms resembles the geodesic domes popularized by architect Richard Buckminster Fuller. These "Buckyballs" resist heat and act as superconductors. Then, in 1991, a researcher at the Japanese technology company NEC discovered the carbon nanotube, which confers great strength without adding weight. Novel nano materials have been reported at a feverish pace ever since.

With these engineered nanoparticles—not even getting into the more complex nanomachines on the horizon—we can deliver drugs to specific cells, "cloak" objects to make them less visible, make solar cells more efficient, and manufacture flexible electronics like e-paper.

In the household realm, nanosilica makes house paints and clothing stain resistant; nanozinc and nano–titanium dioxide make sunscreen, acne lotions, and cleansers transparent and more readily absorbed; and nanosilicon makes computer components and cell phones ever smaller and more powerful. Various proprietary nanoparticles have been mixed into volumizing shampoos, whitening toothpastes, scratch-resistant car paint, fabric softeners, and bricks that resist moss and fungus.

A recent report from an American Chemical Society journal claims that nano–titanium dioxide (a thickener and whitener in larger amounts) is now found in eighty-nine popular food products. These include: M&Ms and Mentos, Dentyne and Trident chewing gums, Nestlé coffee creamers, various flavors of Pop-Tarts, Kool-Aid, and Jell-O pudding, and Betty Crocker cake frostings. According to a market report, in 2010 the world produced 50,000 tons of nano–titanium dioxide; by 2015, it's expected to grow to more than 200,000 tons.

At first some in the scientific community didn't think that the unknown environmental effects of nanotechnology merited CEINT's research. "The common view was that it was premature," says CEINT's director, Mark Wiesner. "My point was that that's the whole point. But looking at risk is never as sexy as looking at the applications, so it took some time to convince my colleagues."

Wiesner's team at CEINT chose to study silver nanoparticles first because they are already commonly added to many consumer products for their germ-killing properties. You can find nanosilver in socks, wound dressings, doorknobs, sheets, cutting boards, baby mugs, plush toys—even condoms. How common is the application of nanoparticles? It varies, but when it comes to socks, for example, hospitals now have to be cautious that the nanosilver in a patient's footwear doesn't upset their MRI (magnetic resonance imaging) machines.

Wiesner and his colleagues spent several months designing the experiments that will help them outline some general ecological principles of the unique nanoverse. He knew they wanted to test the particles in a system, but a full-scale ecosystem would be too big, too unmanageable, so they had to find a way to container-ize nature. They considered all sorts of receptacles: kiddie pools (too flimsy), simple holes in the ground (too dirty, too difficult to harvest for analysis), concrete boxes (crack in winter). Finally, they settled upon wooden boxes lined with nonreactive, industrial rubber: cheap to build, easy to reuse, and convenient to harvest.

They built thirty boxes and a greenhouse to hold them. The large number would make it easier to replicate experiments, and to answer the spectrum of questions being posed by CEINT's interdisciplinary team. The ecologists were interested in community diversity and how the biomass shifts over time. The biologists wanted to know whether the nanoparticles become concentrated as they move up the food chain. The toxicologists wanted to track where the particles went and how fast they got there. The chemists wanted to know about reactivity.

Whatever the goal of the experiment it houses, each mesocosm features a slanted board upon which a terrestrial ecosystem slowly gives way to an aquatic one. It's a lot more complicated than a test tube in a lab, but it remains an approximation. The team had hoped to run streams through the mesocosms, but the computing power and monitoring vigilance necessary to track nanoparticles in the streams proved prohibitive.

In 2011, the team dosed the boxes with two kinds of nanosilver made on campus: one coated in PVP, a binder used in many medicines, and the other coated in gum arabic, a binder used in numerous products, including gummi candies and cosmetics. Both coatings help to stabilize the nanosilver. In some boxes, the researchers let the silver leach slowly into the box. In other boxes, they delivered the silver in one big pulse. In some, they introduced the silver into the terrestrial part of the box; in others, they put the silver into the water.

Then the researchers watched and waited.

Too Small for Poison?

Reading through descriptions of nanoparticle applications can make a person almost giddy. It all sounds mostly great. And the toxicology maxim "Dose makes the poison" leads many biologists to be skeptical of the dangers nanoparticles might pose. After all, nanoparticles are pretty darn small.

Yet size seems to be a double-edged sword in the nanoverse. Because nanoparticles are so small, they can slip past the body's various barriers: skin, the blood-brain barrier, the lining of the gut and airways. Once inside, these tiny particles can bind to many things. They seem to build up over time, especially in the brain. Some cause inflammation and cell damage. Preliminary research shows this can harm the organs of lab animals, though the results of some of these studies are a matter of debate.

Some published research has shown that inhaled nanoparticles actually become more toxic as they get smaller. Nano–titanium dioxide, one of the most commonly used nanoparticles (Pop-Tarts, sunblock), has been shown to damage DNA in animals and prematurely corrode metals. Carbon nanotubes seem to penetrate lungs even more deeply than asbestos.

What little we know about the environmental effects of nanoparticles—and it isn't very much—also raises some red flags. Nanoparticles from consumer products have been found in sewage wastewater, where they can inhibit bacteria that help break down the waste. They've been found to accumulate in plants and stunt their growth. Another study has shown that gold nanoparticles become more concentrated as they move up the food chain from plants to herbivores.

"My suspicion, based on the limited amount of work that's been done, is that nanoparticles are way less toxic than DDT," says Richard Di Giulio, an environmental toxicologist on the CEINT team. "But what's scary about nanoparticles is that we're producing products with new nanomaterials far ahead of our ability to assess them."

As a society, we've been here before—releasing a "miracle technology" before its potential health and environmental ramifications are understood, let alone investigated. Remember how DDT was going to stamp out malaria and typhus and revolutionize agriculture? How asbestos was going to make buildings fireproof? How bisphenol A (BPA) would make plastics clear and nearly shatterproof? How methyl tertiary-butyl ether (MTBE) would make gasoline burn cleanly? How polychlorinated biphenyls (PCBs) were going to make electrical networks safer? How genetically modified organisms (GMOs) were going to end hunger?[1]

The CEINT scientists are trying to develop a library that catalogues all the different kinds of engineered nanoparticles. They're designing methods for assessing potential hazards, devising ways to evaluate the impact nanoparticles have on both terrestrial and aquatic ecosystems, and creating protocols that will help shape environmental policy decisions about nanoparticles.

Wiesner says the boxes in the forest provide "ground truth" for experiments in the lab. Sometimes, he says, environmental research leads to generalizations that become so abstracted that they have no relationship to reality. The example he likes to give is Freon: if you were to study the toxicology of Freon in the traditional way, you'd never get to the ozone hole.[2] "Nature changes things," Wiesner says. "So we need to be able

1. DDT causes birth defects; asbestos causes lung cancer; BPA has been linked to possible toxic effects for infants; MTBE may cause cancer; PCBs have been linked to a number of adverse health effects, including cancer; GMO health effects are currently disputed and controversial.
2. Freon, a coolant, breaks down ozone in the atmosphere, causing a dangerous increase in ultraviolet radiation on earth.

to understand those transformation processes, and we need to understand them in complex systems."

The first large set of CEINT experiments ended about a year ago [early 2012], and the team spent most of last year figuring out where the nanoparticles went, what they did, and how they added up. They superimposed a grid on each box, then harvested the plants and animals section by section. They clipped the grasses, sorted them by type, and ground them up. They took bore samples of the soil, the water, and the rocks. They anesthetized and flash froze the vertebrates. Then they started measuring the nanoparticle concentrations in the plants, the animals, and core-sample slices.

But consider the magnitude of the scientific problems that face the scientists at CEINT, or anyone else trying to answer a multitude of questions as nanotech applications gallop into the market and man-made nanoparticles begin to litter our world. Just try tracking something a billion times smaller than a meter in even a modestly sized ecosystem, say, a small wetland or a lake. Do carbon nanotubes degrade? And if not, then what? And how do you tell the nanotubes from all the other carbon in your average ecosystem? Even if we did regulate nanoparticles, how would we detect them? There's no "nanoprobe" that could find them today, and given the challenges of developing such a thing, the team at CEINT considers it unlikely that there will be one any time soon. Thus, gathering evidence of nanoparticles' effects—whether positive or negative—turns out to be a titanic task. Simply finding them in the experiment samples seems about as complicated as finding that needle in a haystack the size of the Grand Canyon.

Hunting Nanoparticles

Lee Ferguson, a chemistry professor who directs the nanoparticle analysis, meets me in the basement of the CEINT building and leads me on a tour of all the hulking, pricey instruments the researchers use. Despite the cutting-edge aura of this machinery, none of it is fully up to the task of locating and analyzing the proverbial nanoneedle.

"With nanoparticles, we're playing catch-up as a scientific community—not only to ask the right questions, but to have the right tools to investigate them," Ferguson says as he pushes through a door into the first lab. "We were well prepared to answer questions about PCBs—we'd spent half a century refining the chemistry and the instruments that were used to analyze the molecules in those chemicals. But simply *measuring* nanoparticles is a challenge. It's one thing if they're concentrated, but if you're looking for nanoparticles in soil, for instance, you just can't find them."

He spends the next hour showing me how the CEINT team has back-engineered methods to detect and characterize nanoparticles. The fluorometer aims three lasers at carbon nanotubes. Another instrument uses ultrasonic waves to flush out its tiny quarry. Across campus, huge electron microscopes train electron beams on the nanoparticle samples, projecting their images onto a charge-coupled device camera, like the ones used on the Hubble Telescope, and atomic force microscopes form images of them by running a probe over samples like a hypersensitive, high-tech record player.

As the team's methods continue to advance, their experiments have resulted in some surprising data. "After we dosed the water, we took some of it to the lab and exposed fish to it," says Wiesner's research assistant, Benjamin Espinasse. "Some of the particles turned out to be more toxic in the lab. And the reverse also happened: some things didn't appear to be toxic in the lab, but they were more toxic in the boxes. It seems that the organic matter in the mesocosms changed the coatings of the particles, making them more toxic or less toxic," Espinasse continues. "We could never have imagined that."

While CEINT has only published the results of the preliminary mesocosm experiments, the team has been able to make a few conclusions: When the nanoparticles come in a burst, they tend to stay in the soil. But if they bleed into the system slowly, they filter into the water column. Regardless, nanoparticles seem to have a tendency to stick around—that was also the case with DDT.

Meanwhile, CEINT has begun a new set of experiments in the boxes: testing nanoparticles that have been combined with various other substances.

"The materials we see most now are nanomaterials incorporated into other products: textiles, foams, mattresses, nanotubes in display screens," Wiesner explains. "How it will get out into the environment will be very different than just the pristine particle."

And then there are the nanobots to plan for. "As we get closer to even simple nanobots, we will need to understand how to do research on them, too," Wiesner says. Although they remain a marvel of the future, scientists are working toward nanomachines that may someday be able to replicate red blood cells, clean up toxic spills, repair spinal cord injuries, and create weapon swarms to overwhelm an enemy. Researchers are already working on simple versions of nanobots using the chemical principles of attraction and repulsion to help nanostructures arrange and build themselves in a process akin to the way DNA works: a strand of DNA can only split and rebuild in one particular way, and the desired structure is preserved, no matter how many times the DNA replicates.

As if trying to figure out the effects of simple nanoparticles weren't enough of a futuristic challenge, concerns surrounding nanobots that replicate like DNA are so theoretical they're spoken about in narratives resembling science fiction. Sun Microsystems founder Bill Joy famously warned that, if released into the environment, self-assembling and self-replicating nanomachines could spread like pollen or bacteria, and be too tough and too small to stop before invading every part of the biosphere, chewing it up and reducing all life on earth to "gray goo." In nanotech circles, this is called the "gray goo problem," but no one really knows if this vision is prophetic or simply hysterical.

Building Up to the Unknown

Down the basement hallway, postdoc Badireddy motions to me to join him at a computer monitor next to the dark field microscope in his lab. He clicks on a movie he's made from images he's captured. It shows silver nanoparticles interacting with bacteria.

At first, the nanoparticles don't seem to be doing much. Then, all of a sudden, they start to clump to the outside of a bacterium. The nanoparticles build up and build up until the bacterium's cell membrane bursts. Then the nanoparticle clumps dissolve into small units before clumping back up again and attacking more bacteria. "The whole cycle happens in about thirty minutes," Badireddy says. "It's so fast. If you leave the nanoparticles overnight, when you come back in the morning, all the bacteria are ground mush."

If you're looking for stink-free athletic socks, maybe this is a good thing. But could that same process someday turn out to have some sort of nasty biological effect? We just don't know yet.

"The fact that they re-cycle suggests they might persist for a long time," Badireddy says as we watch the movie a second time. "They might enter the food chain. And then, who knows what will happen?"

VIEWPOINT

"Nanotechnology applications will consume less energy and material, generate less waste and pollution while giving the same or even more benefits."

Nanotechnology Can Be Beneficial for the Environment

Veranja Karunaratne, Nilwala Kottegoda, and Ajith de Alwis

Veranja Karunaratne is the science team leader at the Sri Lanka Institute of Nanotechnology; Nilwala Kottegoda is senior lecturer at Sri Lanka's University of Sri Jayewardenepura, and Ajith de Alwis is a professor of chemical and process engineering at Sri Lanka's University of Moratuwa. In the following viewpoint, the authors argue that nanotechnology can help to clean drinking water, increase fuel efficiency, and reduce or reverse environmental degradation in numerous ways. They note that care must be taken to ensure that nanotechnology itself is environmentally safe, but they express optimism about nanotechnology's potential environmental benefits.

As you read, consider the following questions:

1. What do the authors identify as some applications of nanotechnology to remove pollutants from water?

Veranja Karunaratne, Nilwala Kottegoda, and Ajith de Alwis, "Nanotechnology in a World Out of Balance," *Journal of the National Science Foundation of Sri Lanka*, vol. 40, no. 1, 2012, pp. 3–8.

2. According to Karunaratne, Kottegoda, and Alwis, what materials are being used as nanosensors and why?
3. What issues do the authors suggest that life-cycle assessment of nanoparticles should focus on?

As the world population marches towards the 9 billion mark by 2050, factors critical for the sustenance of the ecosystems will come under increasing stress. Having crossed the 7 billion figure in 2011, the 9 billion mark may well be reached much earlier based on population predictions depending on advances in science and behavioural changes. How humanity will address the depletion of resources crucial to our survival will have a bearing on life style, societal values and peace on the planet. Mankind appears to have tipped the scale in favour of population versus resources, probably for all time, and the balance of resources and their use is no longer in our favour. In April 2005, the Millennium Ecosystem Assessment carried out by the United Nations indicated that "*. . . the ability of ecosystems to sustain future generations can no longer be taken for granted*". In the same year, in a significant development, the United Nations in its Millennium Project Report addressed the potential of nanotechnology for sustainable development. [Researchers Fabio] Salamanca-Buentello *et al.* in their [2005] assessment of nanotechnology for developing the world have listed 10 areas for nanotechnology development, aligned with the Millennium Development Goals (MDGs).

As science and technology are crucial to development, nanotechnology as an emerging technology must inevitably address problems of sustainable development created by earlier technologies in the past two hundred years, on one hand, and those that the new technology will generate on the other. This article highlights some critical issues and prioritizes applications of nanotechnology, which can contribute to sustainable development, in the light of particular problems faced by the emerging economies.

Nanotechnology and Sustainability

Nanotechnology can be defined as research and development at the atomic or molecular scale and involves manipulating and manufacturing structures less than 100 nm [nanometers (billionths of a meter)] across. If nanotechnology is to lead the way to sustainable development, then it must fulfill the needs of the current generation without depleting the opportunities of the future generations. Currently there is increasing awareness of the role of nanotechnology as an enabling technology rather than an original technology. Thus, in many examples the nano-component will be a crucial part of a more complex product. Therefore, nano-enabled components will continue to arise in energy technology, information and communication technology and biotechnology. Importantly, according to [researchers T.] Fleisher and [A.] Grunwald all these technologies with their own sustainability issues make cross connections, facing head on societal acceptance or rejection. There is a prevailing consensus among scientists and engineers that nanotechnology applications will consume less energy and material, generate less waste and pollution while giving the same or even more benefits—the classical situation of more from less. In addition, there is reasonable potential on the one hand for more advanced countries to reduce the environmental footprints of their industrial processes and for the developing countries to address their critical sustainability issues on the other.

In this backdrop it is crucial for the developing world to ask how nanotechnology can address the areas identified by the [2002] United Nations Report of the World Summit on Sustainable Development, which need urgent attention: water, agriculture, nutrition, health, energy and the environment.

Water and Energy

Water: Oceans, saline ground water and saline lakes, contain 97.5% of the total amount of water of the planet. Of the remaining 2.5% of fresh water, only 1.3% is available as surface fresh water, the rest being hidden away in ground water, glaciers and ice caps. Of this meager amount of fresh water, nearly 74% is present as ice or snow. Thus, understanding how little is available for human consumption places pollution of water bodies in a catastrophic perspective. Highlighting the seriousness of the water shortage issue, some [such as scientist S.N. Kulshreshtha in 1998] have predicted that "*by 2025 more than half of the world population will be facing water-based vulnerability*". The three major types of contaminants in drinking water are halogenated organics including pesticides, heavy metals and microorganisms. The high surface area to volume ratio of nanoparticles increases the availability of atoms and molecules for adsorption of pollutants. Some notable applications are magnetic nanoparticles and titania [titanium oxide] nanoparticles for removal of arsenic, silver nanoparticles supported on alumina [aluminum oxide] for removal of pesticides and halogenated organics, hydrous polymer based iron oxide nanoparticles for removal of arsenic, chromium, vanadium and uranium and more recently the use of heavy metals for the removal of organic pollutants.

Energy: If new oil supplies are not harnessed, by 2020 the Middle East will control 83% of global oil supplies, and by 2070, there may be no more cost effective oil supplies available. On the other hand, worldwide energy demand is expected to increase by 2% per year until 2035. Ironically over 2 billion people in the developing world have limited access to energy. In addition, since the highest growth rates are also in regions of high fossil fuel usage, the carbon dioxide emissions are expected to outpace energy consumption. The climate watchers constantly worry about what the tipping point of atmospheric carbon dioxide concentration is. In harnessing sunlight for electric power, the currently used photovoltaic technologies are of limited use because of low conversion and high cost. Nanostructured photovoltaic devices using quantum dots, which allow sunlight to be harnessed from a broader range of wave lengths can dramatically reduce cost. Though highlighted early, these processes are yet to show promise in scaled up systems.

Although hydrogen is an alternative to fossil fuels, its formation, storage and conversion to electricity are facing technological challenges. However, in the use of water as a renewable resource to produce hydrogen, the use of nanophoto catalysts have shown promise. It is estimated that such new processes cannot be expected to be in operation until about 2035.

Agriculture

Agriculture and nutrition: The neglect by governments and international agencies of agriculture relevant to the poor, the current worldwide economic crisis, and the significant increase of food prices in the last several years have made close to a billion people, mostly in the developing world suffer due to malnutrition. One of the major problems in agriculture is the loss of the macronutrient nitrogen to the environment from urea used in fertilizer applications. This loss of nitrogen, exceeding 50–60% in the form of urea, is due to the conversion to water soluble nitrates, gaseous ammonia and incorporation into the soil by microorganisms. Mitigating the loss of nitrogen is one way of reducing the cost of food production. However, there has been little research into increasing the efficiency of nitrogen use. Owing to the high surface area to volume ratio of nanoparticles, nanofertilizers will enable the uptake of fertilizer by plants in a slow and sustained manner, which would be more efficient, lead to cost savings and less environmental damage than even polymer-coated conventional slow release fertilizers.

In other applications, pesticides bound to nanoparticles effect timed-release. Nanobiosensors are being developed for detecting harmful pathogens such as *E. coli* [bacteria]. Bionanocomposites, which are hybrids between a biopolymer such as cellulose, clays such as montmorillonite and a plasticizer such as glycerol, when used in packaging increases the shelflife and protects food as well. Bioactive food additives such as probiotics, prebiotics, vitamins and flavanoids can be encapsulated in bioactive packaging and released when needed, into the food products.

Environment and Health

Environment: Having altered one half of the planet's land surface, humanity is in dire straits. According to the United Nations estimates, the amount of wastewater produced annually is about six times more than what is available in all the rivers of the world. Pollution of rivers and lakes from chemical substances (including agricultural chemicals) and eutrophication (including abnormal growth of toxic algae) coupled with water shortages and tropical forest destruction is more widespread now; recently the United Nations Environmental Programme stated that "*the human population is living far beyond its means and inflicting damage on the environment that could pass points of no return*". In addition, air pollution due to increased levels of SO_2 [sulfur dioxide] and suspended particulate matter is rising in urban areas of the developing world. It has been predicted that to reverse climate change, greenhouse gas emissions must be reduced by 50% by 2050. On the other hand, it has been hypothesized that while air pollution levels might go up as a developing country undergoes industrialization while increasing its agricultural production, this trend will be mitigated as the gross domestic product (GDP) increases.

The promise of nanotechnology in addressing environmental pollution related problems is predominantly in the

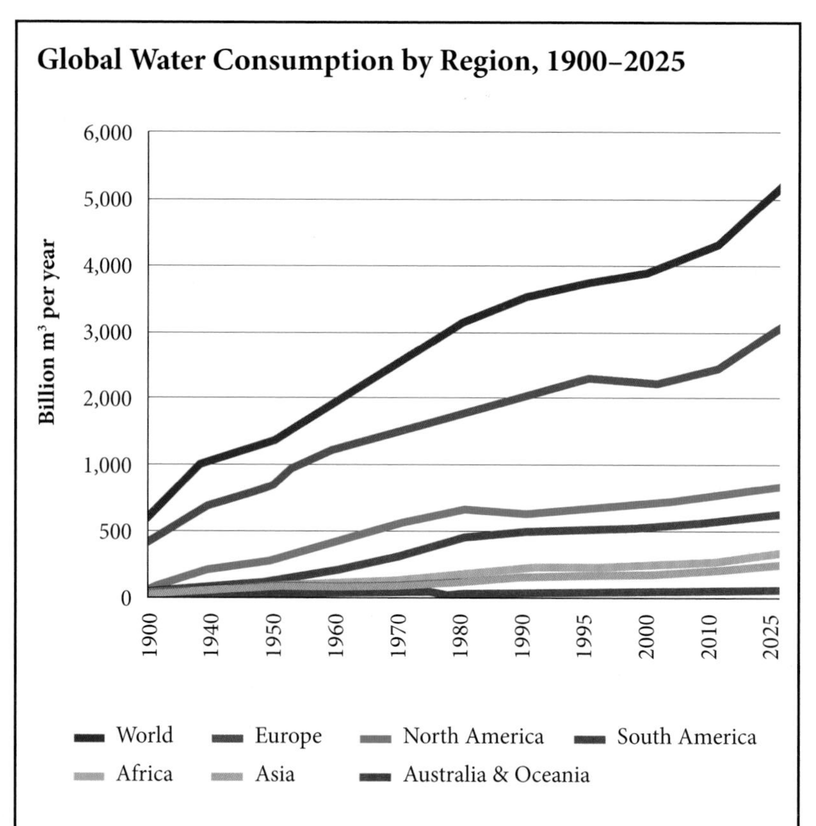

TAKEN FROM: miriamr, "Assignment 5: Sustainable Thinking Through the Eyes of Michelle Kaufmann," *MR7UJ*, November 8, 2011. http://mr7uj.wordpress.com.
"Exhibitions from the Umweltbundesamt—Sustainable and Rational Use of Water and Energy—Examples from Germany—Drinking Water—a Scarce Resource." Steigen Sie Ein: Das Umweltbundesamt—Für Mensch Und Umwelt. Web. November 20, 2011.

area of nanosensors. A variety of nanomaterials such as gold nanoparticles, carbon nanotubes, magnetic nanoparticles and quantum dots are increasingly [being] used as biosensors to detect pollutants because of the unique physical, chemical, mechanical, magnetic and optical properties, which aid in the enhancement of selectivity and sensitivity of detection. In another noteworthy application, liposome based biosensors have been successfully employed for the detection of organophosphorous pesticides such as dichlorvos and paraoxon at very low concentrations. A key thrust area of nanomaterial based biosensors is the development of single molecule biosensors and high throughput biosensor arrays. It is reasonable to assume that such biosensors will be broadly applied to environmental monitoring in the near future.

Medicine: In the United States, about 75% of the manufactured prescription drugs are synthetic. The remaining 25% are derived from natural sources and they rely on organic solvents for extraction and purification. Therefore, the entire global pharmaceutical industry is dependent on the petrochemical industry and when the global competition for oil increases, healthcare for the majority of the developing world will be undermined. Nanotechnology has shown promise in making medicines more effective and low cost, by assembly and immobilization of biomolecules in a synergistic manner. Nanomedicine is defined broadly as either [Britain's Royal Society and Royal Academy of Engineering stated in 2004:] "*use of molecular tools and knowledge of the human body for medical diagnosis and treatment*" or [as researchers M. Sato and T.J. Webster stated in the same year:] "*one that makes use of physical effects occurring in nanoscale objects that exist at the interface between the molecular and macroscopic world in which quantum mechanics still reigns*".

The areas where there is active research and development in nanomedicine are theranostics, targeted drug delivery and regenerative medicine. Theranostics is a fusion of diagnosis and therapy, which leads to better treatment of disease. Nanoparticle-based imaging and therapy are on the verge of entering clinical trials. In a recent finding, gold nanoparticles were delivered to target cells and intracellular plasmonic nanobubbles were optically generated and controlled through laser fluence [that is, the flow of concentrated light over time]; significantly, the plasmonic nanobubbles were tuned in within cells for non-invasive high-sensitive imaging at lower fluence and disruption of cellular membrane at higher fluence. In targeted drug delivery, the pharmaceutical agent is delivered specifically to the diseased cell. Thus, small doses of medicine can be used at just the right place leading to potential cost reductions and fewer side effects. Regenerative medicine uses nanoparticles containing gene transcription factors and other modulating molecules that carry out the reprogramming of cells *in vivo* [in the living organism].

Specific to the developing world, nanobiotechnology has the capability to address three of the United Nations Millennium Development Goals: reducing child mortality, improving mental health and combating HIV/AIDS, malaria and other diseases. However, in comparison to the total pharmaceutical and medical device market, nanomedicines are just emerging and research into the modification of nanoscale carriers remains to be done in order to know more about circulation lifetime, biodistribution and penetration of biological tissues.

Benefits of Nanomaterials

As is seen from the foregoing, nanotechnology can make a paradigm shift to make a difference in solving problems created by previous technologies. However, as a new technology, nanotechnology must become sustainable for it to reach the society at large. Therefore, life cycle assessment (LCA) of nanoparticles and nano-enabled products are important in finding answers to issues such as: (a) How do life cycles of products/devices using nanomaterials compare to those made by conventional materials particularly in the area of energy consumption; (b) What particular phases in the life cycle use the highest amount of energy; (c) Identification of particular end-of-life management issues specific to nanomaterials such as recovery, reuse and recycling; (d) Identification eco-toxicity and human toxicity of nanomaterials.

We must come to terms with the inevitability that manufactured nanomaterials and nanostructures will enter our natural world sooner or later, where several types of nanoparticles have shown unintended consequences. For example, silver nanoparticles, which are bacteriostatic [germ-stopping], may destroy beneficial bacteria important for breaking down organic matter in waste treatment plants or farms. Similar concerns have been expressed about TiO_2 [titanium dioxide] and carbon nanotubes. Aerosols resulting from nanoparticles and their manipulation, the resulting agglomerates and their degradation aerosols and suspensions should be cleared of any potential harm to humans and the ecosystem. If we rely only on exposure controls, such attempts will fail in the long term. Therefore, research must strive for performance without toxicity with the implicit assumption that innovation is not attractive enough until we reach that point. The recent announcement that the Continental Western Group [insurance companies] "*will no longer issue insurance coverage for research and development work on carbon nanotubes until their toxicity has been determined*" is noteworthy. Because of the complex and emerging nature with high social cost, nanotechnology must employ a holistic model where risk based and application based research must be integrated, proactively minimizing health and ecological risks.

It has been recommended that public participation with nanotechnology should be 'upstream' in nature, reflecting its occurrence before commercialization in real-world applications and undoubtedly before significant social controversy, as was the case in genetically modified foods. Significantly, for the first time in the history of science, with respect to nanotechnology, scientists and citizens are engaged in healthy public debates over the new technology. Risk perception analysis indicates that the technology's acceptability will depend upon people's perceptions of both benefit and risk, with the balance between the two depending upon the particular technology or the context within which judgments are formed. Interestingly, nanotechnology surveys in the United States and United Kingdom show two clear findings. The first is that most people know little or nothing about nanotechnologies. Second, notwithstanding this, many feel that nanotechnology's future benefits will outweigh its risks.

Nano-sustainability

Nanotechnology, as it forges ahead, can make a significant impact on addressing the sustainability crises faced by the emerging economies. In addition, it is highly conceivable that the large majority of nanomaterials containing products that reach the market will fulfill the standards of efficacy and safety, assuring that toxicity assessment and environmental impact audits will closely follow innovation. In the end, scientists and engineers who envision and practice nanotechnology must chart a course which leads both to technological advancement and sustainability. Through these exciting yet challenging times, the developing world must prioritize the application of nanotechnologies, which lead to sustainability, halting further erosion of the ecosystem.

Viewpoint 3

> *"'Downsides' to nanotechnology are rarely acknowledged, while 'benefits' claimed are often exaggerated, untested, and are, in many cases, years away from realisation."*

Nanotechnology's Environmental Benefits Are Overstated

International POP's Elimination Network and the European Environmental Bureau

The International POP's Elimination Network (IPEN) is a global network of nongovernmental organizations working to eliminate phosphorous organic pollutants (POPs). The European Environmental Bureau (EEB) is Europe's largest federation of environmental organizations. In the following viewpoint, these organizations argue that any environmental advantages of using nanotechnology are offset by the fact that nanomaterials are energy intensive to produce and have unknown environmental side effects. The authors conclude that environmental challenges can only be solved through social and political commitment, not through new, experimental, and often untested nanotechnologies.

As you read, consider the following questions:

1. Why do the authors believe that nanotechnology will not result in cleaner production?
2. What are the limitations of solar nanotechnology, according to IPEN and the EEB?
3. Why do the authors argue that nanotechnology is less useful in Bangladesh than old sari cloth?

Nanotechnologies are presented as providing unprecedented technological solutions to many environmental problems including climate change, pollution and clean drinking water. Proponents claim that it enables economic growth through better products and new markets while dramatically reducing our ecological footprint. However there is emerging evidence these claims do not provide the whole picture, with serious environmental risks and costs being trivialised or ignored.

Any reductions in environmental impacts or apparent reduction of our ecological footprint, achieved by nanotechnology applications, need to be carefully assessed against the possibility that the environmental costs of nanomaterials production (such as increased energy and water demands) and broader environmental costs outweigh the potential environmental gains for the environment. These 'downsides' to nanotechnology are rarely acknowledged, while 'benefits' claimed are often exaggerated, untested, and are, in many cases, years away from realisation.

Our concerns about the potential negative environmental impacts and costs are made worse by the apparent reluctance of governments to develop appropriate and responsible oversight mechanisms in a timely fashion. Below, we develop in more detail our concerns and propose solutions.

Claims of Environmental Benefits

The OECD [Organisation for Economic Cooperation and Development] suggests that nanotechnology offers environmental benefits in the following principle areas: cleaner production, pollution reduction, and other environmental benefits. However we question nanotechnology's capacity to deliver; in each case the claims are not borne out by reality, and environmental costs are consistently ignored.

Cleaner or Dirtier Production?

Claim: Nanotechnology will deliver cleaner production (e.g. through green chemistry; synthesis and processing of nanoscale materials that will reduce consumption of raw materials and natural resources such as water and energy, and improved chemical reactions and catalysis).

Reality: In addition to nanomaterials fabrication requiring large amounts of water and energy, the chemicals required are often highly toxic, as are many nanomaterials themselves. The concept of 'safety by design', widely promoted, is an illusion without a proper life cycle analysis and validated nano-specific risk assessment methodologies which may be 15 years away.

Energy Saving or Demanding?

Claim: Nanotechnology will deliver applications to reduce energy consumption (e.g. through efficiencies in production, improved energy storage, generation and conservation).

Reality: Manufacturing nanomaterials and nano-devices (including nanomaterials to be used in energy generation, storage and conservation applications) is extremely energy-intensive. Early life cycle assessments shed doubt on the claim that nano-applications will save energy.

Broader Environmental Benefits or Costs?

Claim: Nanotechnology will deliver other environmental benefits (e.g. environmental remediation and monitoring, water filtration, and reduction of agricultural pollution).

Reality: There is no full ecotoxicological profile for any of the nanomaterials available today and the existing scientific results identify potential serious health and environmental concerns. Much more research and ecotoxicological modelling is therefore required before we should consider large-scale environmental release of nanomaterials for use in remediation or other purposes. Nanotechnology has the potential to deliver useful water treatment in some areas. However, even if disregarding potential human toxicity issues, there is a real danger that other water treatment methodologies, including effective, community-controlled methods will be sidelined as priority is given to patented, corporate controlled nano-water treatment applications.

In agricultural applications, even if smaller quantities of nano-chemicals are used in agriculture, because of their far greater potency, this could still pose a greater toxicological burden. Furthermore, use of nano-pesticides in agriculture will entrench our chemical dependence at a time when there is growing recognition and action to limit use of chemicals altogether.

Various aspects of this reality are detailed below together with concrete proposals.

Energy Costs and Toxicity

Nanotechnology proponents have claimed that nanomaterials will lower energy and resource use. This is because small quantities of more potent nanomaterials can theoretically accomplish the tasks of much larger amounts of conventional materials, and because materials such as carbon nanotubes are predicted to enable lighter industrial components whose use will require less energy. However engül et al. (2008) found that the manufacture of nanomaterials has an unexpectedly large ecological footprint. This was related to: highly specialised production environments, high energy and water demands of processing, low product yields, high waste generation, the production and use of greenhouse gases such as methane and the use of toxic chemicals and solvents such as benzene.

In a separate life cycle study of carbon nanofibre production, [V.] Khanna et al. found [in 2008] that their potential to contribute to global warming, ozone layer depletion, environmental or human toxicity may be as much as 100 times greater per unit of weight than those of conventional materials like aluminium, steel and polypropylene.

Nanomaterials are likely to be used in far smaller quantities than conventional substances, so a life cycle assessment of the products they are used in would give a more accurate impression of total energy and environmental impacts. Nonetheless, these early findings led scientists to conclude that any environmental gains of nanomaterials may be outweighed by the environmental costs of production.

Nanomaterials themselves constitute a new generation of toxic chemicals. As particle size decreases, in many nanomaterials the production of free radicals increases, as does toxicity. Test tube studies have shown that nanomaterials now in commercial use can damage human DNA, negatively affect cellular function and even cause cell death. There is a small but growing body of scientific studies showing that some nanomaterials are toxic to commonly used environmental indicators such as algae, invertebrate and fish species. There is also evidence that some nanomaterials could impair the function or reproductive cycles of earthworms which play a key role in nutrient cycling that underpins ecosystem function. Most recently, disturbing new evidence has shown that nanomaterials can be transferred across generations in both animals and plants.

Furthermore, even if used in smaller quantities than conventional chemicals, nanomaterials may have a greater toxicological burden. In 2006 the Woodrow Wilson International Center for Scholars' Project on Emerging Nanotechnologies (PEN) estimated that 58,000 metric tons of nanomaterials will be produced world-wide from 2011 to 2020. PEN stated its concerns that given the potency of nanomaterials, this could have an ecological impact equivalent to 5 million metric tons—or possibly even 50 billion metric tons—of conventional materials.

Solar Energy

Proponents predict that eventually nano-solar panel efficiency will reach 60% (as opposed to around 40% for conventional panels). Today's figures are less impressive. Nanoparticles such as titanium dioxide, silver, quantum dots and cadmium telluride have been used to increase the efficiency of thin film solar cells and gains, to date, have been modest. For instance, Nanosolar, a US firm, produces thin film cells of up to 14% efficiency and claims to be nearing economic production at US$1/watt. However conventional wafer-based crystalline silicon panels remain much more efficient at around 25%, and are also much cheaper. While it is very difficult to compare the cost per watt, European figures for "conventional" solar power systems are around US$0.50/watt.

Nano-solar applications have permitted the production of much more flexible solar panels, and 'reel to reel' printing of panels, which are both distinct advantages. However many of nano solar's more transformational predicted applications, such as energy generating plastic-based paint that can harvest infrared (non-visible) light, are still at an exploratory research stage and remain wholly unproven.

As yet there is no life cycle assessment of nano solar products, so it is unclear whether in order to produce solar energy, large amounts of energy are required in their manufacture.

The Bangladesh Sari Filter

In Bangladesh, where annual flooding often contaminates nearly all surface waters and where over half of the tube wells are severely contaminated with arsenic and fluoride, villagers have been trained to make a reasonably effective filter out of a minimum of eight layers of a folded sari [traditional Indian dress]. Actual scientific controlled tests have verified the efficacy of these low-tech "sari filters." It turns out that older saris work better than ones made of new cloth, because after several launderings the thread fibers tend to become soft and loose, reducing the pore size compared with pore size on new sari cloth. The folded sari filters are held snugly over the neck of a large water jug as it is dipped in a river or pond until filled. After each use, the sari is first rinsed out in the source water, followed by a rinsing in filtered water, then laid out in the sun for further drying and natural UV [ultraviolet] sterilization.

Caution: The use of sari filters is not 100 percent safe. In controlled tests, the method reduced cholera infections by 52 percent, and a large number of mothers using sari filtration perceived a significant decline in the incidence of diarrhea within their families. It is better than nothing, but if you have other more sure-fire treatment options, I suggest you use them.

Matthew Stein,
When Disaster Strikes: A Comprehensive Guide for Emergency Planning and Crisis Survival, *2011.*

What is known is that many thin film technologies are using nanoparticles that pose potentially serious toxicity problems (e.g. cadmium, quantum dots, silver and titanium dioxide nanoparticles).

Carbon Nanotubes

Carbon nanotubes are already being used to reinforce specialty parts of planes and cars and high performance plastics, in fuel filters, electronic goods and carbon-lithium batteries. Their future use has been predicted to enable super lightweight planes and cars that will use much less fuel, dramatically reducing the environmental costs of air travel. They are also mooted for use in textiles, pharmaceuticals, food packaging and a range of other applications.

Using nanotechnologies to fabricate materials that are lighter and stronger than conventional materials, as in the case of carbon nanotubes, translates to clear fuel efficiency gains in cars or planes. Using nano-sized catalysts in car engines (e.g. substances that speed chemical reactions) results in using 70–90% less of the same catalyst in bulk form. Storage capacity, lifetime and safety of batteries are also said to benefit from nanotechnologies. However there are still no product life cycle assessments that tell us whether or not the energy savings made in product use exceed the energy demands of nanomaterials manufacture.

There are also serious concerns about nanotubes' health and environmental risks, in particular, that some carbon nanotubes can cause asbestos-like health harm if inhaled. In 2004, the United Kingdom's Royal Society and risk specialists at the world's second largest reinsurance agent Swiss Re warned that nanotubes may behave like asbestos once in our lungs. Since then, a series of experiments have demonstrated that when introduced into the lungs of rodents, certain carbon nanotubes cause inflammation, granuloma development, fibrosis, artery 'plaque' responsible for heart attacks and DNA damage. Two independent studies have shown that some carbon nanotubes can also cause the onset of mesothelioma—cancer previously thought to be only associated with asbestos exposure.

A new study has found that two types of carbon nanomaterials—C70 fullerenes and multi walled nanotubes

(MWNT)—delayed rice flowering by at least 1 month. They also reduced significantly the yield of exposed rice plants (C70 reduced seed set by 4.6%, MWNT by 10.5%). Seeds exposed for only 2 weeks to C70 fullerenes passed these onto the next generation of seeds. Exposure to carbon nanotubes also makes wheat plants more vulnerable to uptake of pollutants. Carbon nanotubes pierced the cell wall of wheat plants' roots, providing a 'pipe' through which pollutants were transported into living cells.

Rice and wheat are staple crops which feed a large proportion of the world's people. At a time of unprecedented global food crisis, these preliminary studies suggest that carbon nanomaterials could reduce yields of one of the world's most important staple crops and leave another more vulnerable to pollutant uptake.

Water Treatment

Proponents of nanotechnology-based water treatment technologies have claimed that they will be cheaper, more durable, and more efficient than those used currently. Nanotechnologies commercially available or under development include nano-membranes, nano-meshes, nano-fibrous filters, as well as nano-ceramics, clays and adsorbents, zeolites and nano-catalysts. Depending on the technology used they can perform similar functions to conventional methods. However, in addition to raising new safety concerns, their manufacture requires sophisticated technological capabilities, currently only available in specialised facilities, mostly in the developed world. This would continue to leave communities reliant on the ongoing willingness to trade of distant water treatment companies, or on technological charity.

A case in point is a pilot project in Bangladesh on an effective and affordable means to reduce cholera bacteria in local water. The project trialled the use of old Sari [a traditional Indian woman's dress] cloth (folded four times) and it proved a simple, affordable, and reportedly successful method to remove 99% of cholera bacteria from the water. While nanotreatment could additionally allow the filtration of salts and some other substances, it would also take the control of this technology away from the local people.

There is concern that deployment of nano-water treatment technologies may increase the market access of private, profit-driven companies in the critical area of water services. General Electric, Dow Chemicals, Siemens and others have billion dollar stakes in the water market, and have made large investments in nanotechnology-based water treatment research. Nanotechnology will do nothing to redress the economic and political factors the UN World Water Development Report has cited as key reasons for a lack of water access around the globe.

Nano Will Not Solve Everything

Nanotechnology is the latest technological innovation promising to cure many human health and environmental ills. In dealing with nanotechnology in isolation, the risk is of focusing only and too closely on the technology-related impacts (including materials behaviour). Nanotechnology's development stems from an approach that identifies technological innovation as a potential solution to existing problems while providing economic benefits.

Tensions and disagreements arise around the potential benefits of developments such as nanotechnologies when proponents make exaggerated claims about these benefits, whilst overlooking some serious and chronic potential negative impacts.

Nanotechnology, like biotechnology, goes beyond our knowledge of natural systems and cycles, and our ability to monitor or control unintended negative effects. As we continue to develop market applications that go beyond our knowledge on basic natural support systems, the tensions and disagreements mentioned earlier will only continue to increase. This leads to societal unrest as the public is less able to participate in societal decision-making due to their lower level of understanding of the issues being discussed, and their level of trust of public authorities and corporate interests is further eroded.

Better Governance Is Needed

Better governance of technological innovations is fundamental if we are to reduce these societal tensions, and help to guide innovation in publicly acceptable areas. Technological innovation is seen as a means of progress, and a potential source of solutions to environmental problems, but not if it creates problems in areas where we have less scientific knowledge or if it simply shifts them to other known areas—e.g. from energy consumption to pollution.

Technology must operate in the service of society, which means that it needs to be controlled and guided by societal structures. Public debate is needed on acceptable developments of technologies, and on responsibility for damage. Key industrial and research policies should include elaborated sustainability objectives (beyond 'reduced environmental impact') and use sustainability assessment of technologies as a tool to identify more acceptable technological developments.

The Wrong Fix

In the context of nanotechnologies, early evidence of the much greater energy demands of producing nanoparticles, the significant quantities of potentially toxic waste their production generates, and the ecotoxic behaviour of many nanoparticles themselves has cast doubt on industry claims that nanotechnology offers 'green' solutions to the current ecological crises.

In many ways, nanotechnologies are an example of attempted technological-fix to problems that in reality require

2. Why would desalination be especially helpful in Senegal, according to the author?

3. Why does Sanderson suggest that decentralized nanotech water treatment might be able to play an especially large role in the developing world?

We're a thirsty species. Humans can't survive without fresh, clean, drinking water, yet we sprang to life on a planet where 97.5% of water is useless to us.

A Tiny Solution to a Big Problem

What's left for us to drink is becoming more and more polluted by agriculture, industry and poor water-management. By 2030, 3.9 billion people (47% of the predicted population) won't have access to clean water.

There is a tiny solution to this large problem: nanomaterials can strip water of toxic metals and dangerous organic molecules, or turn salt water into fresh water. There are also plenty of other nanotech solutions in development.

"Nanotechnologies that have the best chance are ones we can integrate into existing systems," says Mamadou Diallo, an environmental engineer at both the California Institute of Technology and Korea Advanced Institute of Science and Technology. That means, for example, membranes enhanced with nanoparticles that can slot seamlessly into water treatment plants.

The Nametech project, which is co-funded by the European Commission and the University of Applied Sciences Northwestern Switzerland, is enhancing filters already used in water treatment plants with nanoparticles that do specific jobs.

"We're adding a wide range of nanoparticles," says project manager Thomas Wintgens of the University of Applied Sciences Northwestern Switzerland in Muttenz. These include:

- Biomagnetite, an iron mineral, to get rid of chlorinated organic molecules and some toxic metals.
- Silver to kill bacteria.
- Nanoparticles of titanium dioxide to break down common organic contaminants such as hormones, pharmaceuticals, or manure—all they need to operate is some light to shine on them when they are in the water.
- Titanium dioxide, which is already widely used in paints and sunscreens so, in principle, the technology is cheap.

Nametech is running a small pilot plant to test the membranes. Each 20cm [centimeter] module can process around a cubic metre of water every hour. But, like other new technologies, it needs to be proven beyond the lab.

Rob Lammertink of the University of Twente, the Netherlands, says there is interest from industry for nanotechnology water treatments, but it is still early days. He heads the nanotechnology in water group of a large consortium, NanoNextNL, and predicts that, perhaps in five or 10 years, nanotech water treatments might be used on a large scale.

Other scientists have put the conservatism of the water industry aside, and are thinking smaller to make sure people don't go thirsty.

Cleaning Water with Nanonets

In South Africa, the humble teabag has inspired a way to clean water 1-litre at a time. In the mouth of an ordinary drinking bottle sits a teabag-like net that is a nanotech marvel.

Developed by Eugene Cloete at Stellenbosch University in South Africa, the inside of the biodegradable teabag is coated with thin water-soluble polymer nanofibres that have been impregnated with anti-microbial agents and spun into a fine mesh.

The material filters out most contaminants—up to 99.99% of bacteria. The "tea leaves" inside the bag are activated carbon, which can suck out heavy metals and other contaminants.

As yet the tea bag remains a prototype, the final version, intended for consumers, is still being developed by the company AquaQure. But there is already much hope that this filter could make a big difference to the lives of people who do not have easy access to clean water.

Cleaning up dirty water isn't the only way to quench the world's thirst. Diallo says that producing fresh water out of the world's plentiful supply of salty water, a process called desalination, will be made more efficient and cost effective with nanotechnology.

It could be of huge benefit in countries such as his native Senegal, where over-exploitation of groundwater means that ever-deeper aquifers need to be drilled. Deeper aquifers invariably lead to more brackish water.

Desalination is expensive and needs lots of energy. Reverse osmosis, the favoured current technology, uses high pressures to pump contaminated water across a membrane. "At the moment we extract clean water from seawater—we need to extract the salt instead," says Diallo. "We can't do this without advanced nanomaterials."

Water produced from the world's cheapest desalination plants cost about 31p [pence, British cents] a cubic metre at the moment. But things could be cheaper.

Put two metal plates into salty water, for example, and apply a voltage across them, and the salt will start to separate from the liquid. The positively-charged half of the salt molecules (known as ions) gets attracted to the negatively-charged metal plate and vice versa.

Coat the metal plates with nanomaterials and cycle the voltage across them, and the salt ions can be collected and removed relatively efficiently. Nano-engineered carbon and carbon nanotubes are being examined as candidates, with the potential to cut desalination costs by 75%.

Diallo says that a capacitance device such as the one described above is at least 10 years away from being available on an industrial scale.

But more decentralised water treatment might allow nanotechnology to play a bigger role, in the developing world, for example, where large-scale water distribution centres and networks of pipes do not already exist.

Nanotech desalination and treatment devices could go straight to point of use, or be used in small-scale or emergency situations. "Maybe nanotechnology will level the playing field," says Diallo, and give everyone a clean glass of water to drink.

Viewpoint 5

> *"Nanotechnology has the potential to contribute to efforts to reduce harmful greenhouse gas emissions and therefore assist in responding to climate change."*

Nanotechnology May Provide Innovative Solutions to Climate Change

Miguel Esteban, Christian Webersik, David Leary, and Dexter Thompson-Pomeroy

David Leary is a Senior Lecturer in the Faculty of Law at the University of Technology, Sydney, Australia. Miguel Esteban is a Project Associate Professor in the Graduate Program in Sustainability Science-Global Leadership Initiative (GPSS-GLI) at the Graduate School of Frontier Sciences at the University of Tokyo. Christian Webersik is an Associate Professor in the Department of Development Studies at the University of Agder, Norway. Dexter Thompson-Pomeroy is a student at Columbia University in the City of New York. In the following viewpoint, the authors discuss the potential of nanotechnology in the development of efficient hydrogen powered vehicles, cheaper solar power technology, and a new generation of batteries and supercapacitors

Miguel Esteban, Christian Webersik, David Leary and Dexter Thompson-Pomeroy, "Nanotechnology," *Innovation in Responding to Climate Change: Nanotechnology, Ocean Energy, and Forestry*, UNU-IAS, 2008, pp. 10–19.

(devices for storing and releasing electricity). For hydrogen powered fuel cells, the role of nanotechnology is to increase the surface area of the catalyst that separates the electron from the proton of the hydrogen atom by nanosizing the catalyst. However, the production of hydrogen for the fuel cell may produce greenhouse gas emissions. Nanotechnology is being used to improve the efficiency of existing silicon photovoltaic cells by depositing and baking two-micrometer thick layers of silicon on glass to create more efficient crystalline silicon. Nanotechnology has also been used to improve the negative electrode material in lithium-ion batteries, resulting in double the capacity and 1.5 times the power.

As you read, consider the following questions:

1. According to a United Kingdom government report referenced by the authors, in what areas does nanotechnology have the potential to contribute to efforts to reduce harmful greenhouse gas emissions?
2. According to Esteban, Webersik, Leary, and Thompson-Pomeroy, what is the most significant role of nanotechnology in the move toward the hydrogen economy?
3. According to the authors, what is cadmium telluride, what is it used for, and what are the advantages and disadvantages associated with its use?

Nanotechnology is best described as a 'platform technology'. Nanotechnology will not by itself have a dramatic impact on climate change, but its incorporation into larger systems, such as the hydrogen based economy, solar power technology or next generation batteries, potentially could have a profound impact on energy consumption and hence greenhouse gas emissions.

A recent [in 2008] study by Zäch et al. highlights that in the last decade there has been a very rapid escalation in scientific interest in the potential for nanotechnology to provide tools to tackle energy and environment related issues. . . . [T]here has been a significant increase in the number of scientific publications dealing with the potential of nanotechnology, especially in the research on fuel cells, hydrogen and photocatalysis.

Nanotechnology and Greenhouse Gases

A recent report commissioned for the United Kingdom government recognises nanotechnology has the potential to contribute to efforts to reduce harmful greenhouse gas emissions and therefore assist in responding to climate change in a range of areas including:

- the development of efficient hydrogen powered vehicles;
- enhanced and cheaper photovoltaics or solar power technology;
- the development of a new generation of batteries and super capacitors (i.e. devices that can store and subsequently release electricity) which could make the more widespread use of electric cars a reality;
- improved insulation of buildings;
- fuel additives that could enhance the energy efficiency of motor vehicles.

In a similar vein, a recent study by the United Nations Environment Programme (UNEP) highlights that nanotechnology offers significant new means for transforming energy production, storage and consumption (especially in the fields of solar energy) and better storage for emission-free fuels.

The following discussion concentrates on the role of nanotechnology in innovation in three of these broad categories, namely the development of efficient hydrogen powered vehicles, enhanced and cheaper photovoltaics or solar power technology, and the development of a new generation of batteries and supercapacitors. The reason for this is because in many respects the ongoing R&D [research and development] and actual commercialisation of these technologies are interlinked. For example, the full scale rollout of hydrogen powered vehicles is dependant on the development of new fuel cell technology; and some (but not all) current R&D on fuel cells draws on advances in photovoltaics. These three areas of nanotechnology are also of significance because they provide numerous examples of nanotechnology R&D that has reached the stage of prototypes and or commercial production.

Nanotechnology and the Hydrogen Economy

Nanotechnology plays a crucial role in generation, storage and use of hydrogen as a fuel source. Hydrogen has the potential to replace traditional hydrocarbons [that is, oil, coal, natural gas, and so on] as a major source of energy. The most significant role of nanotechnology in the move towards the hydrogen economy is in the development of hydrogen fuel cells. Fuel cells are electrochemical devices that convert a fuel such as hydrogen or methanol directly into electricity. A recent study describes how a fuel cell operates as follows:

> Fuel cells use catalytic reactions to generate electricity directly from a chemical fuel source. Hydrogen fuel cells operate thus:
>
> - A catalyst splits hydrogen into a proton and an electron.
> - A membrane selectively allows the proton to travel through it whilst preventing the electron from doing so, so that the electron travels through a copper wire to generate an electrical current.
> - A second catalyst on the other side of the membrane combines the proton with the electron and oxygen to form water . . .

> As a general rule, the larger surface areas, the more active the catalyst. The catalytic activity can be maximised by nanosizing the particles of the catalyst. . . .

Nanosizing the catalyst is considered as key to the development of efficient hydrogen fuel cells.

In theory, a fuel cell is similar in structure to a battery, but it does not run down nor need re-charging as long as fuel is supplied. But significantly, conversion of the fuel to energy takes place without combustion and is therefore highly efficient, clean and quiet.

However, it is important to note that hydrogen is a carrier of energy, not a source of energy. As such the use of hydrogen fuel cells is not necessarily carbon neutral. As the hydrogen for fuel cells has to be produced from other sources of energy, this will result in greenhouse gas emissions. The overall impact of hydrogen fuel cells on green house gas emissions will depend very much on the source of energy used to produce the hydrogen. There are examples of R&D utilising nanotechnology, however, that are seeking to get around this limitation. For example, the United Kingdom based company Hydrogen Solar is "developing a solar cell that splits water into hydrogen and oxygen using nanostructured materials".

While finding a carbon neutral way to generate hydrogen is one of the main challenges for the growth of the hydrogen economy, this limitation has not deterred automobile manufacturers from investing vast sums of money on R&D in relation to the development of hydrogen fuel cells. . . . [There are] numerous examples of R&D on hydrogen fuel cells for cars by leading manufacturers. It is clear from this data that innovation in hydrogen fuel is a significant area of R&D for many companies. Many of these cars are still in the prototype or design stage. However, there are now signs that this technology has gone beyond this stage with the first such cars appearing on the market. For example, in June 2008 the Honda FCX Clarity went into production and has gone on limited commercial lease in Southern California, USA. Developments in nanotechnology were crucial to the development of the technology embodied in the Honda FCX Clarity.

Nanotechnology and Solar Energy

Generating photovoltaic energy involves converting light into electrical energy, and is achieved through the use of semiconductors or photovoltaic solar cells. These cells are generally encapsulated in water-tight modules for protection from moisture and impact and the resulting assembly is typically referred to as a solar panel or module.

In 2005, annual sales of photovoltaics technology exceeded US$10 billion and the industry is currently undergoing a rapid period of growth unparalleled in its history. This is due in large part to the fact that "photovoltaic technologies offer a potentially unlimited source of emission free, renewable energy by converting sunlight into electricity."

Nanotechnology is widely used in current R&D in photovoltaics. Some of the main areas of research include: nanoparticle silicon systems; mimicking photosynthesis; nanoparticle encapsulation in polymers; use of non-silicon materials such as calcopyrites to develop thin film technology; molecular organic solar cells; organic polymer photovoltaic systems; development of single walled nanotubes in conducting polymer cells; III–V nitride solar cells; flexible film technology; and development of novel nanostructured materials.

Improving Existing Photovoltaics

While nanotechnology is relevant across a wide range of R&D on photovoltaics, there is now considerable focus on the role of nanotechnology in improving the efficiency of existing silicon photovoltaic panels, which are the most common type of photovoltaic panel in use today. There are several different types of photovoltaic panels such as crystalline and noncrystalline or amorphous silicon photovoltaic panels. Each of these photovoltaic panels differs in their efficiency in terms of converting light energy into electrical energy. Crystalline silicon, while more efficient than amorphous silicon, is also more expensive. There are also concerns about the availability of high grade silicon due to increased demand.

Nanotechnology is a central part of on-going R&D aimed at circumventing these problems. One such approach that has attracted considerable attention is the so called Crystalline Silicon on Glass approach. This approach involves depositing a very thin layer of silicon, less than two micrometres thick, directly onto a glass sheet whose surface has been roughened by applying a layer of tiny glass beads. Heat treatment in an oven then transforms the silicon into crystalline form. The resulting layer is then processed using lasers and ink-jet printing techniques to form the electrical contacts needed to get the solar-produced electricity out of the thin silicon film.

Much of this technology was pioneered by the Australian company Pacific Solar. In 2002, Pacific Solar produced a small Crystalline Silicon Glass module (660 cm2) which set the then world record for solar conversion for thin-film crystalline silicon. In 2004, Pacific Solar sold its rights in this technology to the German company CSG Solar AG. CSG Solar AG now manufacturers and markets Crystal Silicon on Glass Modules.

Using Alternate Materials

Another area of R&D has focused on improvements to photovoltaic cells using alternate materials such as cadmium telluride. Cadmium telluride is a crystalline compound that can be deposited in a very thin layer on glass as a substitute for silicon. The major advantage of this technology is that it is considerably cheaper than silicon based technologies. However, there have been some concerns expressed about possible environmental health and safety problems, especially at the end of the life cycle of products incorporating cadmium telluride.

Numerous other companies are also involved in R&D relating to photovoltaics and solar technology involving nanotechnology. This includes some of the world's largest companies such as DuPont and General Electric, to mention just two. While much of this nanotechnology R&D is focused on improving the efficiency of solar cells, other innovative solutions are being pioneered by lesser known companies such as Nanosolar, which markets itself as the vanguard of a third generation or third wave of solar power.

The Next Generation of Batteries

The first rechargeable battery was the lead-acid battery which was invented in 1859 by French Physicist Gaston Planté. This was followed shortly thereafter in around 1900 with the invention of nickel-cadmium batteries. These two technologies dominated the re-chargeable battery market for much of the 20th century and are still in use today. More recently, a by-product of the space race in the mid 1960s was the development of the nickel-metal-hydride batteries which, from the mid 1990s, have been widely used in consumer electrical appliances such as laptop computers and mobile phones.

The next generation of batteries, and those most relevant to responding to climate change, will be re-chargeable batteries better suited for use in electric cars and other vehicles. Nanotechnology is at the core of mainstream R&D in relation to the next generation of re-chargeable batteries.

Initial work on batteries for use in cars, especially as used in hybrid vehicles, focused on adapting nickel-metal-hydride batteries used in appliances such as laptops and mobile phones. Hybrid vehicles already on the market, such as the Toyota Prius, use nickel metal hydride power cells/batteries.

Lithium-Ion Batteries

This R&D continues, but more recently considerable focus has been placed on the potential of lithium-ion batteries. One such example is the R&D of the Japanese car manufacturer

Main Application Areas for Nanotechnology Relevant to Climate Change Mitigation

The hydrogen economy	Hydrogen as an energy source Hydrogen generation via electrolysis Hydrogen generation from photolysis Hydrogen fuel cells for use in transport (e.g. cars and buses) Hydrogen storage Light metal hydrides Carbon nanotubes storage Molecular sponges
Fuel efficiency	Fuel additives to catalyze fuel efficiency and reduce emissions Cerium oxide powders Cerium salts Improved lubricant additives to minimize corrosion and energy performance Nanodetergents to improve engine performance Nanostructured coatings for turbines Catalytic converters
Photovoltaics/ Solar energy	Nanoparticle silicon systems Mimicking photosynthesis Nanoparticle encapsulation in polymers Calcopyrites Molecular organic solar cells Organic polymer photovoltaic systems Single walled nanotubes in conducting polymer solar cells III-V nitride solar cells Flexible film technology Novel nanostructured materials

Note: Collated and adapted from material presented in Oakdene Hollins Ltd., "Environmentally Beneficial Nanotechnologies: Barriers and Opportunities," Report for the Department for Environment, Food and Rural Affairs (UK), May 2007.

TAKEN FROM: Miguel Esteban, et al., "Innovation in Responding to Climate Change: Nanotechnology, Ocean Energy and Forestry," United Nations University Institute for Advanced Studies (UNU-IAS), 2008, p. 11.

Main Application Areas for Nanotechnology Relevant to Climate Change Mitigation (continued)

Energy storage	Energy storage for transport
	Electric and hybrid cars
	Supercapacitors
	Electric trains, trams and trolley buses
	Batteries for portable consumer information and communication technology (e.g. laptops and mobile phones)
Insulation	Insulation for buildings (to save on heating and cooling)
	Foam insulation
	Nanogels
	Glass fibers
	Glass
	Vacuum insulating panels

Note: Collated and adapted from material presented in Oakdene Hollins Ltd., "Environmentally Beneficial Nanotechnologies: Barriers and Opportunities," Report for the Department for Environment, Food and Rural Affairs (UK), May 2007.

TAKEN FROM: Miguel Esteban, et al., "Innovation in Responding to Climate Change: Nanotechnology, Ocean Energy and Forestry," United Nations University Institute for Advanced Studies (UNU-IAS), 2008, p. 11.

Nissan. Nissan has recently developed a new laminated lithium-ion battery for electric vehicles. According to Nissan it is the same size as a conventional car battery, but has double the capacity (140Wh/kg) and 1.5 times the power even after 100,000 kilometres usage over five years. The result is double the driving distance, achieved with no increase in battery load. Utilizing mainstream nanotechnology R&D techniques, higher power and higher battery capacity have been achieved through modification of the negative electrode material. This increases energy density and reduces electrode resistance due to nano-level electrode design. This technology is due to be launched onto the market in 2009.

Nissan is not the only automobile company that has been conducting nanotechnology R&D to develop next generation battery technology for use in electric vehicles. Mitsubishi has developed and has commenced manufacturing advanced lithium ion batteries for electric vehicles for launch in 2009. Mitsubishi and GS Yuasa Corporation have formed a joint venture company to develop and build large format lithium ion batteries for automotive applications. This involves an initial investment of US$30 million to install equipment at Yuasa's main plant to produce up to 200,000 lithium cells annually. The batteries to be produced by the joint venture are based on the "LIM series" of Large Lithium-ion batteries manufactured by GS Yuasa which reportedly have ten times the capacity of those already used in hybrid electric vehicles. Mitsubishi also plans to supply these batteries for use in electric vehicles manufactured by other auto-makers.

In a similar vein, electronics company Sanyo is developing nickel-metal hydride batteries for hybrid electric vehicles. These batteries have been adopted by Ford Motors in the USA and Honda Motors in Japan. Sanyo is also developing next-generation nickel-metal hydride batteries with Volkswagen, Germany.

Managing the Risks

While there are potentially many benefits offered by nanotechnology for responding to climate change, there are also emerging concerns about the potential risks that nanotechnologies present to humans and the environment and the ability of current regulatory regimes to sustainably manage those risks. As nanotechnologies are an emergent field of science and technology, it is not yet clear precisely what risks they pose to humans, animal health and the broader environment. As [J.] Kuzma and [P.] VerHage have observed:

> The risks could be practically zero or they could be significant, depending on the properties of a particular product

> and exposure levels. For the most part, no one knows. Few risk assessments have been done that allow one to predict what happens when these very small materials, some designed to be biologically active, enter the human body or are dispersed in the environment.

The most significant issues raised so far relate to the toxicity of manufactured nanoparticles and their ability to enter the human body and reach vital organs via the blood. However, there are still "significant gaps in knowledge about how nanoparticles act, their toxicity and how to measure and monitor nanoparticle exposure."

Clearly many more scientifically rigorous studies and risk assessments still need to be undertaken to confirm or refute these initial concerns, and perhaps more significantly, to clearly delineate the nature and scale of the risks potentially associated with the use of nanotechnology.

What is not clear is whether any of the concerns that have been raised in relation to nanotechnology are at all relevant to the technologies relevant to climate change, including those discussed in this report. This requires further detailed study.

Ethical Issues

Given the sophisticated and expensive nature of nanotechnology R&D, there are also ethical issues raised concerning the ability of less developed countries to benefit from and sustainably manage such advances in technology. What is unclear is whether less developed countries will be able to readily access this new technology, and perhaps more importantly, whether they have the capacity to properly assess and manage potential risks.

The extent to which the public and, perhaps more importantly, civil society (which has a major role to play in shaping public responses and attitudes to nanotechnology) fully understands both the technology that lies behind nanotechnology and the potential risks and benefits offered by nanotechnology is unclear. In some sections of civil society and in the community more broadly, there appears to be an emerging visceral response to nanotechnology which is both sceptical, and in some cases, outright hostile.

In part this is motivated by very genuine and reasonable concerns about the scientific uncertainty surrounding the potential risks to human health and the environment posed by some forms of nanotechnology; in part there is also a lack of understanding of the new technology. Already we are seeing quite emotional comparisons between asbestos [a flame-resistant substance which causes cancer] and genetically modified organisms or GMOs. Whether those concerns are well founded remains to be seen, but for public trust and enthusiasm for nanotechnology to be maintained, it is vital that developments in nanotechnology occur against the backdrop of a robust, transparent, and efficient regulatory regime for nanotechnology.

Internationally there is increasing recognition of the need for closer examination of the regulatory implications of nanotechnology. As one recent author has noted:

> There are two key issues at the heart of regulation of nanotechnology applications and products. Does the nanotechnology create something new and currently unknown to the applicable regulatory regime? Does the unprecedented small scale of the nanotechnology application or product make a currently known material, process or product significantly different, from the perspective of regulatory goals? If the answer to one or both of these questions is yes for a given nanotechnology application, then regulatory changes are likely to be required. If neither of those two conditions exist for a given nanotechnology application, then the existing regulatory framework can effectively handle the application.

More Research Is Needed

As noted above, more detailed research is required on the nature of potential risks associated with nanotechnology before regulators can determine what might be an appropriate regulatory response. So far no country has yet formulated regulations that apply specifically to nanotechnology, although many countries are currently examining proposals for such regulation. One of the few countries that has considered the regulatory implications of nanotechnology in any significant detail is the USA. Thus in early 2007, the US Environmental Protection Agency (EPA) issued a White Paper on Nanotechnology which considers the future role of the EPA in environmental issues that may emerge from current and future developments in nanotechnology. But so far there is no wide ranging proposal in the USA for nanotechnology regulation at the national level, while a number of proposals are in various stages of development at the state level. Similar developments at the national and state and or provincial level are also underway in other developed countries such as Australia and in Europe.

International Regulation

At the international level, the consideration of the regulatory implications of nanotechnology by intergovernmental organisations (especially within the United Nations System) has been at best rudimentary and fragmented, and has so far failed to comprehensively grasp the full range of regulatory challenges posed by nanotechnology across all sectors.

Despite having a wide mandate on a range of environmental issues, the main United Nations organisation dealing with environmental issues, the United Nations Environment Programme, does not yet have a dedicated program or project related to nanotechnology. In 2007, UNEP's fourth annual report on the changing global environment highlighted the urgent need to adopt appropriate assessment and legislative processes to address the unique challenges presented by nanomaterials and their life cycles.

As well as stressing both the potential risks and benefits offered by nanotechnology, the GEO report also highlighted a

"Nanotechnology is not an unqualified environmental saviour nor will its widespread use . . . enable us to pursue 'business as usual' while substantively reducing our environmental footprint.

Nanotechnology Is Unlikely to Provide Solutions to Climate Change

Ian Illuminato and Georgia Miller

Ian Illuminato is a nanotechnology researcher at Friends of the Earth International, an environmental watchdog group, and Georgia Miller is coordinator of the Friends of the Earth Nanotechnology Project. In the following viewpoint, they argue that nanotechnology's potential to reduce greenhouse gas emissions has been severely overstated. For example, they cite the example of solar energy and argue that nanotechnology is less efficient than other solar technologies and possibly less environmentally friendly. They conclude that reduction in energy consumption and a move away from a constantly growing economy is the only real way to reduce greenhouse gas emissions and consequent climate change.

Ian Illuminato and Georgia Miller, *Nanotechnology, Climate and Energy: Over-Heated Promises and Hot Air?*, Friends of the Earth, November 2010, pp. 3–92.

As you read, consider the following questions:

1. According to the authors, how might nanotechnology actually increase use of fossil fuels like oil and gas?
2. Why was the cost advantage of nano-solar panels eroded at the time the authors were writing?
3. What was the argument of the "Prosperity Without Growth" report, as described by Illuminato and Miller?

In a world increasingly concerned about climate change, resource depletion, pollution and water shortages, nanotechnology has been much heralded as a new environmental saviour. Proponents have claimed that nanotechnology will deliver energy technologies that are efficient, inexpensive and environmentally sound. They predict that highly precise nanomanufacturing and the use of smaller quantities of potent nanomaterials will break the tie between economic activity and resource use. In short, it is argued that nanotechnology will enable ongoing economic growth and the expansion of consumer culture at a vastly reduced environmental cost.

Unfulfilled Promises

In this report, for the first time, Friends of the Earth puts the 'green' claims of industry under the microscope. Our investigation reveals that the nanotechnology industry has overpromised and under-delivered. Many of the claims made regarding nanotechnology's environmental performance, and breakthroughs touted by companies claiming to be near market, are not matched by reality. Worse, the energy and environmental costs of the growing nano industry are far higher than expected.

We also reveal that despite their green rhetoric, governments in the United States, Australia, the United Kingdom, Mexico, Japan and Saudi Arabia are using public funds to develop nanotechnology to find and extract more oil and gas.

exposed to sludge, similar to that found in typical waste water treatment plants, four times the typical level of the potent greenhouse gas nitrous oxide is released.

Nanotechnology is not an unqualified environmental saviour nor will its widespread use in everything from socks to face creams enable us to pursue 'business as usual' while substantively reducing our environmental footprint. At best, such claims can be interpreted as the result of wishful thinking on the part of proponents; at worst they can be seen as misleading greenwash.

A Huge Cost

Nanotechnology is a powerful technology that has the potential to deliver novel approaches to the methods by which we harness, use, and store energy. Nevertheless, Friends of the Earth warns that overall, this technology will come at a huge energy and broader environmental cost. Nanotechnology may ultimately facilitate the next wave of expansion of the global economy, deepening our reliance on fossil fuels and existing hazardous chemicals, while introducing a new generation of hazards. Further, it may transform and integrate ever-more parts of nature into our systems of production and consumption. . . .

Nanotechnology and Solar Energy

There is debate about the extent to which nanotechnology offers real breakthrough potential in solar energy. Amidst the hype that nano solar technologies will soon deliver energy at half the price of oil, coal or gas, in 2007 nanotechnology analyst Cientifica's CEO [chief executive officer] warned that the obstacles to scaling up laboratory discoveries were considerable and that a 'reality check' was required regarding its promise. The challenges associated with taking a nano solar lab discovery and scaling it up to deliver a marketable product have proven prohibitive for many companies. A Lux Research analyst has cautioned that even high profile companies making thin film photovoltaics [PVs] who claim to be using nanotechnology to lower costs have struggled to scale up laboratory achievements and to still achieve a functioning product. . . .

Questionable Claims

A group of US researchers has cautioned that amongst the buzz surrounding nano solar are "questionable claims on the scientific facts". They are pessimistic about nano solar's prospects: "nanostructure solar cells are unlikely to play a significant role in the manufacturing of future generations of PV modules". They blame unrealistic assumptions involved in theoretical work and a failure to take into account manufacturing and scale-up constraints for the misplaced hype about nano solar's potential.

One of the key areas where nanotechnology has offered an advantage until recently is in reducing production costs. As a general rule, thin film modules (sets of panels) are lower priced than silicon modules for equivalent energy powers (Solarbuzz 2010). In its October 2010 review of the solar module retail price environment, Solarbuzz found that the lowest retail price for a multi-crystalline silicon solar module was US$1.97 per watt from a US retailer. The lowest retail price for a mono-crystalline silicon module was $2.21 per watt (€1.61 per watt), from a German retailer. The lowest thin film module price was US$1.40 per watt from a US-based retailer (Solarbuzz does make the point that technical attributes and prices are variable).

In spite of this, the cost advantage associated with using thin film nano solar has been eroded in recent months. Falling costs of silicon have lowered the costs of manufacturing silicon cells. Massive investment by the Chinese government to expand significantly its solar production has helped drive the price of solar panels down 40 percent in the past year.

the use of nanofluids and nanocomposites to improve the efficiency of converting heat into electricity is also at a very early stage and faces several technical and design challenges.

Sustainability and Life Cycle Issues

Proponents of thin film nano solar argue that the sector has years of growth before it has to worry about running out of raw materials. However, scarcity analysts have warned that the growth of nano solar may be imminently curtailed due to its reliance on scarce minerals such as indium and gallium, and rare earths such as selenium and telluride. The reserves of both indium and gallium are disputed. However, German researchers suggest that we have less than ten years before we run out of indium. Dutch researchers argue that because thin film nano solar based on cadmium telluride and CIGS is reliant on scarce minerals such as indium and gallium, these technologies will never be able to contribute more than 2 percent of global energy demand, due to resource constraints. They caution that governments should require careful resource constraints assessment before further funding of these thin film technologies: "Large scale government funding for technologies that will remain marginal is not an efficient way to tackle the energy and climate crisis".

The United Nations Environment Programme (UNEP) has warned that despite concern within the high tech sector over scarcity and high prices of minerals such as indium and gallium, only around one percent of these crucial high-tech metals are recycled, with the rest discarded and thrown away at the end of a product's life. UNEP commissioned a report that found that unless end-of-life recycling rates are increased dramatically, specialty and rare earth metals could become "essentially unavailable" for use in high tech products.

Companies such as Walmart have claimed that because thin film nano solar cells contain fewer raw materials, their overall life cycle environmental impact is lower than that of traditional silicon solar cells. However, such claims ignore evidence that the environmental burden and energy costs of producing nanomaterials are very high.

Not More Environmentally Friendly

. . . [A]study in the *Journal of Cleaner Production* assessed the environmental demands and performance of dye-sensitised nano solar cells and fullerene-based organic cells and found that they were not more environmentally friendly than silicon solar for the following reasons:

> . . . high energy and materials inputs in the production of nanoparticles, a relatively low solar radiation to electricity conversion efficiency, a relatively short service life, the use of relatively scarce metals and relatively poor recyclability, if compared with the multi-crystalline Si [silicon] solar cell which currently is the market leader. Moreover, the lack of data and the inability of current methods to handle hazards of nanoparticles generate problems in conducting comparative life cycle assessment of nanoparticulate solar cells.

[One Dutch researcher] observes that "in actual development work [of nano solar] there seems to be no focus on achieving (net) environmental improvement. This is at variance with the attention to environmental improvement in the development of other types of solar cells." This is in direct contrast to the claims made by nano solar companies who promise to create green solutions for energy generation. . . .

Beyond Nanotechnology: Alternatives

In many ways nanotechnology offers the ultimate attempted techno-fix to problems that require integrated social, economic and political solutions. We are concerned that rather than providing real solutions to our most pressing problems, nanotechnologies will underpin a new wave of industrial expansion that will magnify existing resource and energy use and exacerbate environmental destruction.

based on unbounded economic growth was once unthinkable. However, this has been the key proposal from the UK's Sustainable Development Commission's (SDC) "Redefining Prosperity" project and its "Prosperity without growth" report. The report, authored by the SDC's Economics Commissioner Professor Tim Jackson, emphasises that the profits and benefits of growth have been distributed in a massively inequitable manner. It recognises that for poorer countries, higher income levels and greater material prosperity can deliver important health, educational and social outcomes. However, it argues that people in wealthy countries can lead more fulfilling lives and increase their "social prosperity" without further economic growth. This is an important idea whose time has truly come.

The President of the United States and many of his predecessors have attempted to green corporate actions and interests. In President Barack Obama's 2010 Earth Day statement, he mixed the need to safeguard our planet with the country's financial interests: "We have . . . renewed our commitment to passing comprehensive energy and climate legislation that will safeguard our planet, spur innovation and allow us to compete and win in the 21st century economy". Averting dangerous climate change requires us to challenge this core aim to "compete and win in the 21st century economy." Unless governments and industry abandon their commitment to endless economic expansion, no amount of efficiency measures will ever enable us to live sustainably on a finite planet.

Periodical and Internet Sources Bibliography

The following articles have been selected to supplement the diverse views presented in this chapter.

Mike Childs	"Nanotechnology—Proceed with Caution," Friends of the Earth, March 1, 2012. www.foe.co.uk.
eNews Park Forest	"Silver Nanoparticles in Sewage Sludge Found to Disrupt Ecosystems," March 5, 2013. www.enewspf.com.
Environmental Defense Fund	"Nanotechnology and Health," n.d. www.edf.org.
Environmental Protection Agency	"Using Nanotechnology to Detect, Clean Up and Prevent Environmental Pollution," n.d. www.epa.gov.
ETH Life	"Nanotechnology Against Oil Pollution," June 28, 2011. www.ethlife.ethz.ch.
Tiffany Kaiser	"Nanotech Coating Produces Electricity from Sewage," DailyTech, July 23, 2010. www.dailytech.com.
Ken Silverstein	"Nanotechnology: Expanding Clean Energy and Easing Fuel Shortages," *Forbes*, March 5, 2013.
Will Soutter	"Nanotechnology in Agriculture," Azonano.com, December 7, 2012.
Sindy K.Y. Tang	"The Nanotechnology Solution to the Global Water Challenge," Science in the News—Harvard, June 2010. https://sitn.hms.harvard.edu.
Alasdair Wilkins	"Nanotech Tea Bag Creates Safe Drinking Water Instantly, for Less than a Penny," io9, August 13, 2010. http://io9.com.

source of nuclear energy. Technology that could make nuclear weapons safer and more usable could also be applied to nuclear power plants. Indeed, as Kimm Fesenmaier says in a November 15, 2012, essay at the Caltech website, researchers are already trying to use nanotechnology to create radiation-resistant materials for use in nuclear reactors. The intersection of nano and nuclear technology, then, has both great potential and great dangers for the international community.

The viewpoints in this final chapter debate other ways in which nanotechnology may affect international relations, development, and security.

VIEWPOINT 1

> *"Nanotechnology has the potential to dramatically improve the position of the world's poorest people."*

Nanotechnology Could Alleviate Many of the Problems of the Developing World

Jacob Heller and Christine Peterson

Jacob Heller and Christine Peterson work on nanotechnology issues for the Foresight Institute, a California nonprofit organization that promotes transformative technologies. In the following viewpoint, they argue that nanotechnology can provide major benefits for impoverished and developing countries. For example, they say that nanotechnology could reduce production costs, lowering the prices of all goods, and that it could increase agricultural production. The authors warn, however, that if no precautions are taken, nanotechnology's benefits could go mostly to rich nations, worsening rather than alleviating the plight of the poor.

As you read, consider the following questions:

1. What developing countries do the authors single out as being involved in nanotech research?

Jacob Heller and Christine Peterson, "Nanotechnology, Poverty, and Disparity," Foresight Institute.

Governmental Spending in Nanotechnology for Top Ten Countries

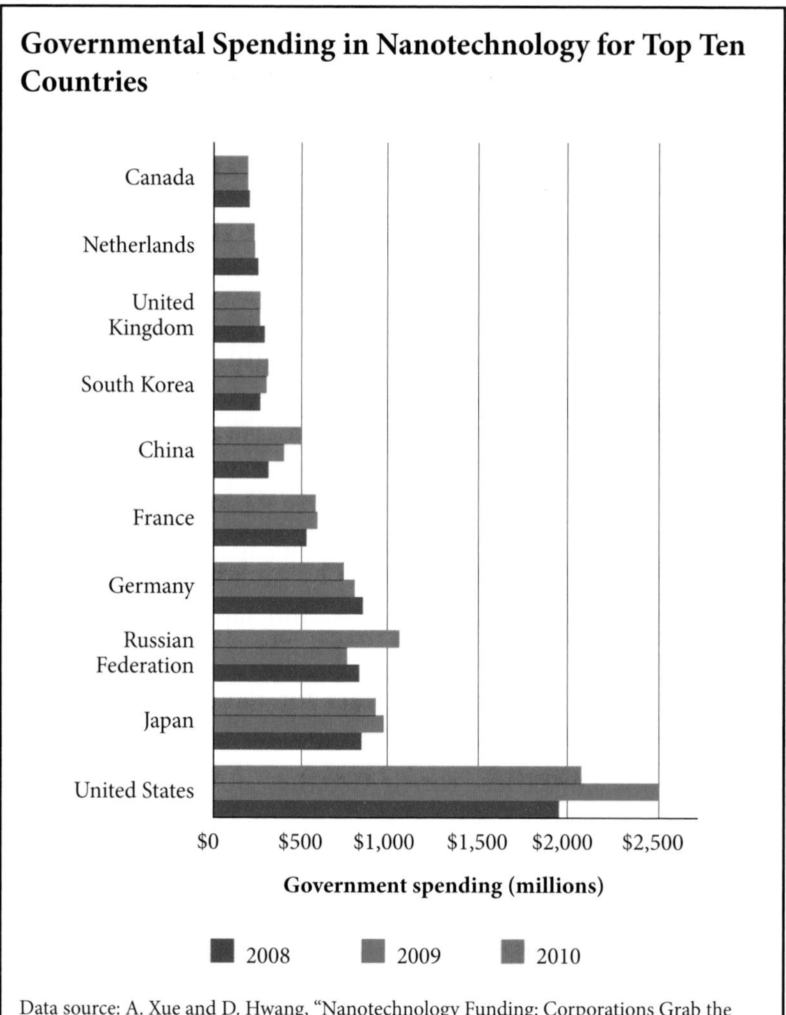

Data source: A. Xue and D. Hwang, "Nanotechnology Funding: Corporations Grab the Reins," Lux Research, April 2011.

TAKEN FROM: President's Council of Advisors on Science and Technology, "Report to the President and Congress on the Fourth Assessment of the National Nanotechnology Initiative," April 2012, p. 14.

Going the Way of GMO

However, similar hopes were put forth for other technologies in the past, but the benefits to the poor have often been delayed and in some cases have never materialized. In the 1980s, there was great hope that biotechnologies, especially genetically modified organisms (GMOs), would solve hunger problems in the developing world. Over a quarter of a century later it is apparent that, while some GMO advances may have helped the poor, most of the benefits accrued in the developed world, where they are most widely grown and consumed. Many of the innovations that were supposed to dramatically improve the quality of life in the developing world, such as plants that could grow in the arid deserts of Africa, have not yet appeared.

The same is currently true with pharmaceuticals. Antiretroviral AIDS medication can substantially increase the quality and length of life for those infected with AIDS, while significantly decreasing the rate of transmission of the deadly virus. However, most of these drugs are held under patents, which raise the price of the drug (because they are being produced by a monopoly) and do not allow developing countries to synthesize their own, cheaper generic versions of the drugs. Because of this, tens of millions of the world's poorest people with AIDS have no access to lifesaving medication. Only recently has this begun to change; more aggressive policy action, taken earlier, could have saved many lives and prevented immense economic losses suffered by societies which can least afford them.

Nanotechnology could easily go the way of GMOs and AIDS drugs, especially if policy action is not taken. In the worst case, it might affect the developing world in an even more serious manner than GMOs and AIDS drugs, since not only would many of the benefits of nanotech innovations be unavailable to the developing world, but the economic gap between the developed and developing world could widen. Nanotechnology benefits come from both the productive process and the final product. Without enough capital and know-how to accumulate and use nanotech-enabled production technologies, the developing world would be outpaced in economic development by the developed world. The great economic disparities created could be highly destabilizing.

There would have to be conscious effort in both the developed and developing world to ensure that the benefits of nanotechnology are spread as widely as possible. Such efforts might include increased investment into encouraging world nanotechnology research and development, allowing developing countries to have exemptions from specific nanotech patents, innovative intellectual property efforts similar to biotech's Cambia, [a nonprofit that seeks to make biotech technology widely available] and substantial resource and knowledge sharing between the developed and developing worlds. Without action today, it is unlikely that the many benefits nanotechnology can provide to the developing world will arrive in time for many of those who need them most.

Viewpoint 

> *"Developing countries that embrace nanotechnology should not overlook possible risks and must regulate products that contain nanoparticles."*

More Regulation and Risk Assessment of Nanotechnology Is Needed in Developing Countries

Alok Dhawan and Vyom Sharma

Alok Dhawan is principal scientist and Vyom Sharma is a senior research fellow at the Nanomaterial Toxicology Group, CSIR-Indian Institute of Toxicology Research, Lucknow, India. In the following viewpoint, they argue that there is too little focus on the potential risks of nanotechnology, especially among researchers in the developing world. They say that nanotechnology might have more risks in developing countries because of lower levels of health among the population, as well as other factors. But developing nations put little effort into researching the risks of nanotechnology, preferring to invest in research on applications. The authors conclude that a better balance is needed.

Alok Dhawan and Vyom Sharma, "Address Risk of Nanotech Toxicity," SciDev.Net, August 25, 2011. http://www.scidev.net/en/new-technologies/nanotechnology/opinions/address-risk-of-nanotech-toxicity-1.html.

As you read, consider the following questions:

1. How does gold's reactivity change when it is converted to a nano-form, according to Dhawan and Sharma?
2. What rules regulating nanoparticles are being proposed by the EPA, as reported by the authors?
3. What was the balance of nanoparticle studies focused on toxicity funded by the Indian government in 2001–2010, according to the authors?

Nanotechnology, the science of manipulating tiny particles less than 100 nanometers in diameter, has found many applications in consumer products, biomedical devices, drug delivery agents and the industrial sector.

In the consumer sector alone, more than 30 countries are manufacturing some 1,300 nanotech-based products, including textiles, food packaging, cosmetics, luggage, children's toys, floor cleaners and wound dressings. The number of such products has increased five-fold in the last five years.

But this rapid growth has also raised concerns about the potential for adverse effects on human health and the environment. Although research on harm remains inconclusive, developing countries that embrace nanotechnology should not overlook possible risks and must regulate products that contain nanoparticles.

Special Properties and Possible Harm

Their small size gives nanoparticles some unusual physical properties, as they have a larger ratio of surface area to volume than bigger particles. This can also make them biologically more active. For example, when gold, usually an inert material, is converted to a nano-form, it acts as a catalyst for chemical reactions owing to high surface reactivity.

This suggests that nanoparticles may interact differently with biological systems, compared with larger particles, and could reach further into the body.

People can be exposed to nanoparticles either directly, such as through nano-based drugs and topically applied cosmetics or sunscreens, or indirectly, for example by inhalation during synthesis of nanoparticles.

A number of studies have documented *in vitro* [in a lab] and *in vivo* [in live organisms] toxicity of exposure to nanoparticles. Evidence suggests they can induce DNA damage, reactive oxygen species, damage to cellular organelles and cell death.

And a study published in the *European Respiratory Journal* in 2009 claimed that seven Chinese workers developed severe lung damage after inhaling polyacrylate nanoparticles produced in their printing factory—the first time that a link was made between exposure to nanoparticles and human illness.

There is currently no mandatory consumer labelling of nanomaterials as potentially hazardous in any country. But governments and scientific bodies in the developed world—including the Royal Society, United Kingdom, and the US Environmental Protection Agency (EPA)—are taking note of the potential hazards and have set up committees to formulate risk assessment guidelines.

For example, under existing regulations, the EPA is proposing rules requiring those that manufacture, import or process two chemical substances—multi-walled and single-walled carbon nanotubes—to submit a notice with information that would help it monitor health or environmental risks.

Similarly, washing machines using silver nanoparticles at the end of the wash cycle are being evaluated by the US government for their environmental safety. In 2005, concerns about toxic effects on microbe populations prompted the temporary withdrawal of a washing machine using silver nanoparticles in Sweden.

India and Nanotechnology

Given India's current state, [as a developing country] how should it invest in nanotechnology? To what extent should it focus on "pro-poor" innovation, producing products that make life better for its rural and urban poor? To what extent should it gear its nanotechnology effort toward producing products to sell in high-income markets? To what extent should it focus on the new consumer class in emerging economies, just out of poverty and ready to buy, as long as the goods purchased are inexpensive? To what extent should it pursue a possible competitive advantage in producer goods for other emerging economies? . . .

To preview our findings, there is scant evidence in the materials we have considered for India's pursuit of either pro-poor or emerging consumer NSE [nanoscience and engineering] strategies. . . . An initial look at company descriptions shows a concentration on intermediate materials and on biomedical applications, where most world effort has been directed toward expensive improvements in affluent-world techniques, not low-cost applications for poor households. A few counterexamples, however, show the capability of large Indian firms to recognize and reach out to new markets and may give a glimpse into potentials for both economic and social development in that direction.

Vrishali Subramanian, Thomas S. Woodson, and Susan Cozzens, "Nanotechnology in India," in Making It to the Forefront, *2012.*

The US EPA has already decided to regulate products containing silver nanoparticles, which are used widely in consumer products and have anti-bacterial properties.

Guidance Is Needed

But developing countries still lack awareness of the potential hazards of nano-based consumer products, and only a few guidance documents are available in the public domain.

A company in India already claims to be the world's largest manufacturer of nanotech-based fabrics. Many other companies that synthesise nanoparticles—for use in cosmetics, for example, or water filtration devices—are emerging in countries such as China and India.

Framing regulations and guidelines for the synthesis, use and disposal of nanomaterials is of great importance for the responsible development of nanotechnology in developing nations. International organisations and developed nations can assist them by sharing scientific data and technologies for assessing environmental and health safety.

And to control occupational exposures, the regulatory framework should include mandatory documentation of the nanomaterials developed and personnel involved, and training workers to take precautions.

Our institute, the Indian Institute of Toxicology Research, Lucknow, has recently published guidance on the safe handling of nanomaterials in research laboratories, a step in the right direction.

But the vast majority of government funding in developing nations is spent on research into the applications, rather than the implications, of nanotechnology.

For example, out of more than 200 research projects funded during 2001–10 by the Department of Science and Technology in India under its flagship Nano Mission programme, only one was directly related to nanoparticle toxicity studies (and was awarded to our institute).

As a result, scientists may fail to identify any impacts of nanotechnology that are specific to populations or the use of a product in poor countries—patterns of environmental distribution and exposure could be different in developing nations.

Current research on nanotoxicity does not take into account how different local environments and populations can influence risk. People in developing countries may be more prone to adverse effects of nanoparticles because of underlying health conditions and malnutrition. Moreover, genetic susceptibility to toxic effects varies in diverse ethnic groups and geographical areas.

The scientific community needs to identify these information gaps before developing regulations and standard methodologies for nanotoxicity assessment.

Viewpoint 3

> *"If any one nation succeeds in cornering the giant's share of the [nanotech] market, it 'would be sufficient to confer global economic leadership on the country.'"*

Asian Nanotech Research Is Threatening to Surpass That of the West

Tom Mackenzie

Tom Mackenzie is a writer for the Guardian, *a major British newspaper. In the following viewpoint, he argues that China is investing huge amounts in research and development of nanotechnologies, including both commercial and military uses. He contends that the United States continues to lead the field but that China is catching up and may reach parity with the West in the near future. If China manages to dominate nanotechnology innovation, he concludes, it could significantly shift the international balance of power in the world.*

As you read, consider the following questions:

1. What is revolutionary about the nanospeaker that Mackenzie describes?

Tom Mackenzie, "China's Giant Step into Nanotech," *Guardian*, March 25, 2009.

2. How might the economic crisis stimulate China's nanotechnology industry, according to Shoushan Fan, as cited by the author?
3. What are some military uses of nanotechnology that Mackenzie quotes Tim Harper on?

Seated inside one of China's most advanced science laboratories, two PhD students dressed from head to toe in protective white suits listen intently to Mariah Carey's pop classic "Hero." It is not the song, but the millimetre-thin, transparent strip making the sound that captures their attention—a nano-speaker they hope will revolutionise where, and how, we listen to music.

China's Sweeping Nanotech Programme

"This is cutting edge," says Professor Shoushan Fan, director of the nanotechnology lab at Beijing's prestigious Tsinghua University. Without a cone, magnet or amplifier, the speaker, which looks like little more than a slim film of see-through plastic, can be used to transform almost any surface into an auditorium. It is made from nanocarbon tubes which, when heated, make the air around them vibrate, producing the sound. "The speaker's bendy and flexible," says Fan. "You could stick it to the back window of your car and play music from there."

Fan's nano-speaker is just the tip of the iceberg in China's sweeping nanotech programme, which has the potential to transform its export-based economy and nearly every aspect of our lives, from food and clothes to medicine and the military.

Nanotechnology—the manipulation of matter on an atomic scale to develop new materials—is an industry predicted to be worth nearly 1.5tn [trillion] pounds [Sterling] by 2012, and China is determined to corner the biggest chunk of the market.

Its investment has already surpassed that of any other country after the US. Since 1999, China's spending on research and development (R&D) has gone up by more than 20% each year. A further boost will come from the £400bn [billion] economic stimulus package announced by the Chinese government this year [2009], £12bn of which has been ringfenced [earmarked] for R&D.

The Next Science Superpower?

"The overall trends are irrefutable," says Dr James Wilsdon, director of the Science Policy Centre at the Royal Society, and author of the Demos report "China: The Next Science Superpower?". "China is snapping at the heels of the most developed nations, in terms of research and investment, in terms of active scientists in the field, in terms of publications and in terms of patents."

Fan hopes the economic crisis [which began in 2008 worldwide], which has led to thousands of Chinese factories closing, will force the country to move from the manufacture of low-end products such as toys and trainers [athletic shoes] to more hi-tech goods such as nano-touchscreens for mobile phones. His team is working on a material to replace the indium tin oxide (ITO) used in the kind of touch panels found on BlackBerrys and iPhones. "ITO is very expensive and breaks if bent," he says. "We're developing thin nanotube films to replace ITO. It can bend and it's much cheaper."

China now produces more papers on nanotech than any other nation. Nanotech plants have sprung up in cities from Beijing in the north to Shenzhen in the south, working on products including exhaust-absorbing tarmac [asphalt] and carbon nanotube–coated clothes that can monitor health. Last month [February 2009], researchers from Nanjing University and colleagues from New York University unveiled a two-armed nanorobot that can alter genetic code. It enables the creation of new DNA structures, and could be turned into a factory for assembling the building blocks of new materials.

"There's no end of areas in which nanotech is already being used," says Wilsdon. "It's the product of targeted investment for the development and refinement of novel nanomaterials. And the reason the Chinese focus on that area is because it's closer to the market."

Military Uses

China, like the US, is also assumed to be focusing much of its R&D investment on military applications. "There's a lot of concern about the use of nanotech with weapons," says Wilsdon. "I'm sure China is spending significant amounts of their R&D budget on military uses."

Tim Harper, founder of the nanotech consultancy Cientifica Ltd, says carbon nanotube composites could be used to strengthen armour, that non-scratch nano-coatings are being developed for cockpits, and researchers are trying to find a nano replacement for military-use batteries. "The US is working on all of these things, so I'm sure the Chinese are doing much the same," he says.

Underlying these developments are serious safety concerns. Nanoparticles are so small they are easily inhaled and absorbed through the skin. Dr Andrew Maynard, the chief science advisor to the Project on Emerging Nanotechnologies at the Woodrow Wilson International Center for Scholars in Washington, says that some nanoparticles could be deadly. "Nothing has yet been confirmed, but there are strong suggestions that inhaling these particles could cause lung cancer or lung disease," he says. "If carbon nanotubes behave anything like asbestos, we won't know what the health impacts are for about 20 years, because that's how long it can take from exposure to the onset of the disease."

Most experts agree that a system of stringent safety regulations and comprehensive quality inspection checks is needed

The US vs. China in Nanotech

Beijing has made it clear that it has no intention of missing what could be the catalyst for a new industrial revolution. In fact, [there is] . . . a determined push for China to situate itself at the forefront of nanotechnology. The entire budget for nanotech research in China may be in the range of $300–$400 million, and the National Science Foundation of China funds over 650 projects with "nanotechnology" in the title, according to the Center for Nanotechnology in Society at the University of California, Santa Barbara. The huge Taiwanese electronics manufacturer Foxconn has invested more than $40 million in a nanotechnology center at Tsinghua University, directed by Fan Shoushan. . . .[A] visiting Japanese scientist described it as "the best equipped research center I have ever visited in China."

As a result, China leads the world in some specialized areas of nanoscience and ranks second in the world in the publication of nanotech research papers. Although U.S. spending on nanotechnology totals more than $3 billion, . . . the founder of the U.S. government's National Nanotechnology Initiative, Dr. Mihail C. Roco, has cautioned, "The U.S. does not have the overwhelming advantage we have in other technologies. We have to compete harder."

Adam Segal,
Advantage: How American Innovation Can Overcome the Asian Challenge, *2011.*

before China's nano-coatings, cosmetics and clothes are stocked by supermarkets. "The economic crisis could prove the catalyst that Chinese nanotech companies need to get this system in place," says Harper.

VIEWPOINT 4

> "The very survival of the United States and the rest of the free world depends on . . . nano-weaponry."

Future Wars Will Be Waged with Nano-Weapons

Lev Navrozov

Lev Navrozov is a Russian author, historian, and translator. In the following viewpoint, he argues that nanotechnology will transform warfare, making guns and tanks and traditional weaponry obsolete. He asserts that the United States has been reluctant to pursue nanoweapon development for fear of appearing militaristic and warns that totalitarian countries such as China have no such qualms about nanoweapon development. He concludes that the United States must aggressively pursue the development of nanoweaponry if it is to survive.

As you read, consider the following questions:

1. Why did Eric Drexler say in his speech that developing nanoweaponry was not necessary, according to Navrozov?

Lev Navrozov, "Future Wars Will Be Waged with Nano-Weapons," Newsmax, September 5, 2008.

2. Why in his book did Drexler say that nanoweaponry could be more dangerous than nuclear weapons, in the author's view?

3. According to Navrozov, why do totalitarian countries have an advantage in developing nanoweapons?

In 1986, Eric Drexler published his book about nanotechnology, "Engines of Creation." He also introduced the very words "nano" and "molecular nanotechnology" in their new sense.

I defended Drexler in my articles because Congress made no allocation to his "Foresight Institute," since he was represented by his ill-wishers up to the early 2000s as a charlatan who had invented fantasies like nano and molecular nanotechnology.

Today, just several years later, to ridicule molecular nanotechnology would be like ridiculing higher mathematics.

In its apparent wish not to seem militaristic and receive allocations from Congress, the Foresight Institute held a conference not near its site in California but in Washington, D.C., and invited several congressmen. I was present as a member of the Institute.

Now, the general title of Drexler's book is "Engines of Creation," and only one chapter (Chapter 11) was entitled "The Engines of Destruction." I was interested in this particular chapter, since the very survival of the United States and the rest of the free world depends on superior "engines of destruction," that is, nano-weaponry.

When Drexler finished his presentation (about the "Engines of Creation"), I raised my hand to speak, and I heard the editor of a nano-magazine whispering, in a theatrical manner, say, "Now, run for cover!"

I asked Drexler why in his speech he did not mention the "Engines of Destruction"; that is, nano-weapons for the defense of the United States and the free West in general.

Drexler's answer was that when the engines of creation had been realized universally, the problem of world peace would have also been solved, and so there would be no need for the nano-engines of destruction.

On a more historical note, let us recall that England became in the 17th century a strong military power due to its Industrial Revolution (spinning and weaving machines, Watt's steam engine, the railway locomotive, and the factory system with its assembly lines). Arms that used explosives were called "firearms." That was what war was like for about four centuries, including the past century: steel contraptions blasted out—by means of explosives—bullets, shells, bombs, etc., to kill enemy soldiers and destroy enemy installations.

Nano-weaponry makes it all as obsolete as firearms made bows obsolete in the 17th century.

Originally, Drexler included "Engines of Destruction" in his book but then took it out, possibly for fear of being viewed as a militarist. However, on his Web site, Ray Kurzweil, an admirer of Drexler and a scientist of genius in his own right, published Chapter 11.

In Chapter 11, Eric Drexler writes that nano-weapons "can be more potent than nuclear weapons: to devastate Earth with [nuclear] bombs would require masses of exotic hardware and rare isotopes, but to destroy all life with [nano] replicators would require only a single speck made of ordinary elements." We also read, "A [nuclear] bomb can only blast things, but nanomachines . . . could be used to infiltrate, seize, change, and govern a territory or a world."

The epigraph to "Engines of Destruction," taken from Sir William Perry and dated by 1640, says, "Nor do I doubt if the most formidable armies ever heere [sic] upon earth is a sort of soldiers who for their smallness are not visible."

To compare the size of Drexler's "nano-soldiers" with that of microbes? The unit of molecular nanotechnology is a molecule. Drexler proceeded from the fact that a molecule contains space, which can be filled, thus converting the molecule into a mobile computer and God knows what else. Yet compared with a molecule, a microbe is a giant: Even before Drexler's studies, one nanocentimeter meant one billionth of a centimeter.

All this may seem miraculous in 2008 just as firearms seemed miraculous in 1646. Yet the new epoch has come: The future world war will be a war of nano-weapons, not of firearms.

The advent of the epoch of firearms was fostered by the Industrial Revolution. There is no such nano-machinery revolution that would foster the production of nano-weaponry. My readers ask me where they can see nano-weapons as they can see firearms. Devoted to new weapons in all countries is the book "Oblivion: America at the Brink" by Lt. Col. Thomas Bearden (U.S. Army, retired). Bearden believes that the United States is "at the brink" in this respect. "If we are to survive, we shall need the most strenuous and rapid effort in our history, now."

What about nano-weapons? Bearden's book, published in 2005, does not yet say a word about them.

In a totalitarian country, its owners can allocate as much funds into a military project as is necessary in their opinion to win the crucial war. In a free country today, the decision depends on the electoral majority, on the media, explaining to the majority what should be done, and on the top-level bureaucracy, some of whose members take into consideration their own interests first and foremost.

From what I have seen in the United States in the last decade, the chances of the free world surviving in a modern world war (that is, the war of nano-weapons, not of firearms) requires strong minds, not the attempts to assure men of genius like Drexler that the engines of destruction are just figments of their imagination because they sound militaristic to Congress.

VIEWPOINT 5

> *"There is an urgent need for regulating nano-weapons under the international law of weaponry."*

International Laws Must Be Developed to Regulate Nanoweaponry

Thomas Alured Faunce and Hitoshi Nasu

Thomas Alured Faunce is a professor in the College of Law and the Medical School and Hitoshi Nasu a senior lecturer in law at the Australian National University in Canberra. In the following viewpoint, they argue that dangerous new military nanoweapons are being developed but that there are few regulations for effectively controlling or limiting their use. General humanitarian principles are often difficult to enforce, and it will likely be some time before the international community manages to create a new treaty specifically focused on limiting military nanotechnology, they maintain. Despite the difficulties, however, the authors urge quick movement on nanoweapon regulation in order to prevent the development and deployment of inhumane technologies.

Thomas A. Faunce and Hitoshi Nasu, "Nanotechnology and the International Law of Weaponry: Towards International Regulation of Nano-Weapons," *Journal of Law, Information, and Science*, vol. 20, 2009/2010, pp. 21–54.

As you read, consider the following questions:

1. What is DIME, and why might it violate international humanitarian laws governing weaponry according to the authors?
2. What important defensive applications of military nanotechnology do Faunce and Nasu discuss?
3. What are the two basic principles of international humanitarian law that the authors say are highly relevant to nanoweaponry?

The renewed Israeli military attack in Gaza in early 2009 was widely condemned as contrary to basic principles of international humanitarian law, one notable example being the indiscriminate use of lethal and maiming white phosphorus in densely populated civilian areas. Equally problematic under the international law of weaponry in that conflict, albeit not so widely reported, was the alleged use of a novel weapon called Dense Inert Metal Explosive (DIME). DIME involves an explosive spray of superheated micro shrapnel made from milled and powdered Heavy Metal Tungsten Alloy (HMTA), which is highly lethal within a relatively small area. The HMTA powder turns to dust (involving even more minute particles) on impact. It loses inertia very quickly due to air resistance, burning and destroying through a very precise angulation everything within a four-meter range—and it is claimed to be highly carcinogenic and an environmental toxin. This new weapon was developed originally by the US Air Force and is designed to reduce collateral damage in urban warfare by limiting the range of explosive force. Its capacity to cause untreatable and unnecessary suffering (particularly because no shrapnel is large enough to be readily detected or removed by medical personnel) has alarmed medical experts. DIME (at least on some definitions) may well be a manifestation of a new generation of nano-scale technological impacts upon modern warfare that at present appears to be poorly regulated under international law. . . .

Secrecy and Regulation

The military use of nanotechnology is expanding rapidly, as evidenced by details of the funding poured into military research and development in nanotechnology in countries such as the US, UK, India, Sweden, and Russia. Nano-weapons . . . are an under-regulated form of military technology in international law and this is likely to cause major problems for both civilians and combatants during and after armed conflict. Nano-weapons are hard to define, but encompass not only objects and devices using nanotechnology that are designed or used for harming humans, but also those causing harmful effects in nano-scale if those effects characterise the lethality of the weapon.

Governmental secrecy surrounding military research and development makes it difficult to describe the current level of military applications of nanotechnology with any degree of certainty. Nanotechnology, however, has reportedly found actual or potential military applications for lighter, stronger and more heat-resistant armour and clothing, bio/chemical sensors, lighter and more durable vehicles, miniaturisation of communication devices, conventional missiles with reduced mass and enhanced speed, small metal-less weapons made of nanofibre composites, small missiles and artillery shells with enhanced accuracy guided by inertial navigation systems, and armour-piercing projectiles with increased penetration capability. The development and military application of nanotechnology are thus not confined to defensive capabilities, but encompass offensive 'nano-weapons' including particularly objects and devices using nanotechnology that are designed or used for harming human beings. The definition, effects and impacts of nano-weapons are yet to be comprehensively detailed under any of the existing international legal regimes on weaponry.

Technological developments with novel military applications have always posed challenges to effective international regulation, not least because of the inevitable secrecy during their research and production. International arms control regimes have been set up to regulate the manufacture, deployment, use and monitoring of certain types of weapons with major focus on chemical, biological and nuclear weapons. Recently, however, the application of computing and software innovations to various emerging technologies has led to major changes in the military tactics of developed nations, which may have outpaced existing arms control regimes under international law. . . .

Military Applications

The relevance of nanotechnology to the military resides particularly in its enabling applications in electronics, optoelectronics, and information and communication systems for detecting, preventing and deterring bioterrorism, the latter being a national research priority in developed nations. Nanotechnology thus has a recognised defensive military capability. Standard bioterrorist threats, for example, could involve aerosol attacks on individuals or crowds, 'dirty' bombs and targeted contamination of food sources, each utilising chemical or biological agents of a size, amount or distribution that nanotechnology sensors and computing will greatly assist in uncovering. Bioterrorist threats such as botulinum in milk, or release of pathogenic organisms and biotoxins in the water supply may not themselves involve nanoscale agents, but their detection may require correlation of vast amounts of information beyond the capacity of non-nanotechnology sensing, information and communication systems. Likewise, threat responses to unexpectedly virulent modifications such as mousepox IL-4, or a highly virulent strain of influenza virus (akin to the strain which caused the Spanish influenza pandemic in the winter of 1918–1919 and killed up to 50 million people worldwide), are likely to benefit greatly from defensive nanotechnology surveillance systems. Atlantic Storm, for example, was a simulated bioterrorism exercise based on the deliberate release of smallpox viruses in various European and North American cities. It revealed that many nations had inadequate vaccine stockpiles, response plans, and public health laws to effectively respond. Such exercises have illuminated the need to develop innovative defensive technologies (including nanotechnology) capable of allowing health officials to promptly detect minute amounts of viral loads in widely dispersed locations and effectively communicate the relevant details to public health authorities. States negotiating under the Biological Weapons Convention (BWC) recently emphasised the need for broad-based codes of conduct for both scientists and public health physicians to counter future bioterrorist threats, partly by warning of the professional perils involved in deliberate or inadvertent release of information and substances.

Military applications of nanotechnology will not be confined to defensive capabilities, however. Nanotechnology allows the building of conventional missiles with reduced mass and enhanced speed, small metal-less weapons made of nanofibre composites, small missiles as well as artillery shells with enhanced accuracy guided by inertial navigation systems, and armour-piercing projectiles with increased penetration capability. Although it is still highly speculative, further research could lead to the development of micro-combat robots, micro-fusion nuclear weapons, new chemical agents carried by nanoparticles, and new biological agents with self-replication capability.

Some of the potential offensive military applications of nanotechnology could span several traditional technological compartments and blur the distinction between conventional weapons and weapons of mass destruction. The ability of nanotechnology to design and manipulate molecules with specific properties could lead to biochemicals capable of altering metabolic pathways and causing defined hostile results ranging from temporary incapacitation to death. Nanotechnology could also make it possible to contain and carry a minute amount of pure-fusion fuel safely until released, detonating a micro-nuclear bomb at a microspot. As will be shown below, it is likely that those new weapons would be subjected to prohibition and inspection under existing treaties, as long as currently available chemicals and biological agents are used in nano-size. However, the dual-use potential of nanotechnology and the low visibility of nanoparticles in weapons make it hard to detect their development and use as weapons....

Arms Control Law and Nano-Weapons

Currently there is no international treaty that has specific provisions regulating nano-weapons. Therefore, in order to determine the extent to which nano-weapons are covered by existing international law it will be necessary to examine whether general principles governing weaponry apply, or whether extant arms control treaties impose restrictions by reasonable extension.

States have agreed in a variety of international treaties to specific and express rules on arms control, which apply even in peacetime. Yet, the adoption of treaties to prohibit certain weapons tends to be reactive (rather than preemptive) and limited in scope, and has been largely dictated by considerations of military effectiveness. Thus, states have agreed to ban the use of projectiles of a weight below 400 grams that are explosive or charged with fulminating or inflammable substances, expanding bullets, asphyxiating, poisonous or other gases, biological weapons, chemical weapons, blinding laser weapons, anti-personnel mines, and most recently, cluster munitions. Nanotechnology, if used as an enabling technology for weapons development in these areas, would be regulated at

A Timeline of Some Major Arms Control Treaties

1968—Nuclear Non-Proliferation Treaty (nuclear powers agree to disarm and nonnuclear powers agree not to acquire nuclear weapons)

1975—Biological and Toxin Weapons Convention

1993—Chemical Weapons Convention

1996—Comprehensive Test Ban Treaty (bans nuclear weapons testing)

1997—Ottawa Convention (bans anti-personnel mines)

2008—Convention on Cluster Munitions

Medact, "Disarmament and Arms Control Treaties," www.medact.org.

least in part by the relevant convention. For example, prototype nanotechnology lasers producing megawatts of continuous power are far more powerful than those previously known, and are likely to be subject to the 1995 *Protocol on Blinding Laser Weapons* in the visible region. Nanotechnology can also produce toxic chemicals with novel properties, and may facilitate the development of synthetic organisms with a high degree of lethality. Yet the arms control treaties in these areas were drafted without any consideration of nanotechnological developments.

Defining New Weapons as Nano-weapons

The recent development and deployment of DIME, for example, illustrates the difficulty in defining whether new weapons fall within the nanotechnology category, or within existing rules of international arms control law. DIME was developed at the US Air Force Research Laboratory in order to achieve low collateral damage by producing a highly powerful blast within a relatively small area. Its development originates from depleted uranium research and is the latest innovation in the US military's long-running development of Focused Lethality Munitions (FLM), designed to provide the 'weapons of choice' in targeting terrorists hiding among civilians. Upon detonation, the carbon fibre warhead case disintegrates into minute, non-lethal fibres with little or no metallic fragments, then sprays a superheated micro-shrapnel of powdered (potentially nano-scale) tungsten particles with sufficient penetration mass for disabling the target within a small lethal footprint.

Do Existing Treaties Apply?

Due to the undetectable nature of tungsten micro-particles in human tissue, the question arises whether this weapon falls within the scope of the 1980 *Protocol (I) on Non-Detectable Fragments to the Convention on Prohibitions or Restrictions on the Use of Certain Conventional Weapons* ('1980 *Protocol (I)*'). It appears that the design intent of this weapon meets the threshold for the prohibition, as the primary effect of metal dust sprayed with DIME is to kill, injure, or damage by blast without leaving much trace of fragments. When the 1980 *Protocol (I)* was adopted unanimously, states did not have such weapons in the inventory, nor did they foresee any conceivable use of them in the future. It could well be argued, according to a textual interpretation, that DIME is not prohibited under the 1980 *Protocol (I)*, as micro-shrapnel could still be detectable by X-ray, no matter how difficult might be in practice. Yet, both a contextual and purposive interpretation of the *Protocol* support the case that DIME is prohibited given the potential seriousness of injuries caused by DIME attacks and the difficulty of treatment due to the size of the fragments.

DIME bombs were reportedly employed by Israel during the 2006 conflicts in Gaza and Southern Lebanon, and more recently during the Gaza conflict in January 2009. As Israel is a party to the 1980 *Protocol (I)*, it is arguable that it breached those treaty obligations by employing DIME bombs. Few authoritative allegations, however, have been made against the use of DIME by Israeli forces on such grounds. If DIME is to be considered at least in some respects a nano-weapon chiefly due to the potential nano-scale of powders produced upon impact, this would complicate the assessment of its legality under the existing treaty obligations. . . .

International Humanitarian Law

The international arms control treaties noted above usually concentrate on regulating or prohibiting the specified weapon's construction aims and characteristics. General principles of international humanitarian law, on the other hand, tend to regulate the conduct of warfare by reference to the harmful effects produced by the use of means or methods of warfare. The general principle, for example, that 'the right of belligerents to adopt means of warfare is not unlimited' may have had its roots in compassion and rejection of unnecessary suffering textually manifesting in Ancient Greece and India. No matter how nascent this was as a legal principle before the emergence of modern international law of armed conflict, it has received widespread support amongst the leaders of nations over many years. There is now little doubt about whether this broad statement about the regulation of weaponry is a reflection of 'elementary considerations of humanity'. More specifically, there are two basic principles of international humanitarian law highly relevant to nano-weaponry: one prohibiting the employment of arms, projectiles, or material 'of a nature to cause superfluous injury' (or 'calculated to cause unnecessary suffering'); and the other prohibiting the use of weapons that indiscriminately affect both combatants and non-combatants. . . .

In practice, it is likely to prove difficult to rely on general humanitarian law principles by themselves as laying down a firm legal basis for restricting the usage of nano-weapons outside a specific arms control treaty. In the *Legality of Nuclear Weapons Opinion*, for instance, the International Court of Justice was unwilling to declare the threat or use of nuclear weapons illegal in all circumstances, even though it explicitly acknowledged the applicability of the general humanitarian law principles....

Action Is Difficult but Necessary

The lack of a specific treaty rule of international law governing the acquisition, development or use of nano-weapons, we argue, creates a hiatus where such weapons can be used experimentally and without adequate scrutiny. Although we still have to wait for a full scientific study, there are already warnings regarding the health and environmental impacts of engineered nano-particles used in military contexts.

Because of this uncertain, yet potential risk to human health and the environment, there is an urgent need for regulating nano-weapons under the international law of weaponry. However, to extend the existing international arms regulation to new nano-weapons poses a real challenge for academics, the military, policy-makers and international civil society.

From our analysis two points are clear in this regard. First, despite the normative significance of the international humanitarian law principles concerning weaponry, their practical value in regulating nano-weapons is significantly hampered by indeterminacy, diverse interpretations, and scientific uncertainty that become obvious when the principles are applied to a specific new weapon. Second, the only way to overcome those problems has traditionally been the adoption of a treaty banning specific weapons. However, those treaties are very much the outcome of a process of military evaluation, over which the consideration of strategic military consideration preponderates. Given the military sensitivity of new weapons development and scientific uncertainty that largely remains surrounding the health and environmental effects of nanoparticles, it will be extremely difficult to garner political will sufficient to move states towards the adoption of a specific legally binding treaty to ban nano-weapons.

Regulatory Failure

This 'regulatory failure' in respect of the development, production or use of nano-weapons suggests the value of investigating novel regulatory approaches .... Yet, the key question as to which new regulatory model would effectively prevent people from being exposed to potential health and environmental effects unnecessarily produced by offensive nano-weapons, while facilitating peaceful program of nanotechnology, remains to be answered.... Prompt action by governments is required, as the military use of nanotechnology is rapidly growing.

Periodical and Internet Sources Bibliography

The following articles have been selected to supplement the diverse views presented in this chapter.

Charlie Jane Anders	"Nanotech Could Make Nuclear Weapons Much, Much Tinier," io9, October 9, 2009. http://io9.com.
Fakir Balaji	"India in Danger of Missing 'Nano Bus': PM's Scientific Advisor," TwoCircles.net, July 6, 2011. http://twocircles.net.
Eric Berger	"Has China Already Passed America in Nanotechnology?," *SciGuy* (blog), Chron, November 3, 2009. http://blog.chron.com.
Sujit Bhattacharya and Madhulika Bhati	"China's Emergence as a Global Nanotech Player: Lessons for Countries in Transition," *China Report*, November 2011.
International Food Policy Research Institute	"Agriculture, Food, and Water Nanotechnologies for the Poor," June 28, 2011. www.ifpri.org.
Ineke Malsch	"Can Nanotechnology Really Help End Poverty?," *The Broker*, May 31, 2010.
Jayshree Pandya	"From Nanotechnology to Nano-Defense," International Relations and Security Network, December 10, 2012. www.isn.ethz.ch.
SciDev.net	"China 'Soaring Ahead' in Nanotechnology Research," March 5, 2012. www.scidev.net.
Will Soutter	"Nanotechnology in Chemical Warfare," Azonano, February 16, 2013. www.azonano.com.
Kathy Jo Wetter	"Big Continent and Tiny Technology: Nanotechnology and Africa," Foreign Policy in Focus, October 15, 2010. www.fpif.org.

For Further Discussion

Chapter 1

1. On the basis of the material you have read in the viewpoints in this chapter, do you think science fiction stories about nanotechnology have advanced or damaged the development of nanotechnology? Explain your reasoning.
2. Are people too worried about the dangers of nanotechnology or not worried enough? Use evidence from the viewpoints in this chapter to support your answer.

Chapter 2

1. Do the benefits of using nanotechnology to treat TB outweigh the risks, in your opinion? Explain your reasoning, citing from the viewpoints.
2. Is it correct to say that nanoparticles are linked to Alzheimer's or Parkinson's disease? Explain your reasoning citing from the viewpoint by Azonano.

Chapter 3

1. What are the possible ways in which nanotechnology can help create clean water? What are the downsides of relying on nanotechnology to do this?
2. Has technology ever solved any environmental problems? Depending on your answer to this question, are Illuminato and Miller too pessimistic about the environmental potential of nanotechnology to affect climate change? Or are Esteban and his coauthors too optimistic?

Chapter 4

1. Should the United States work to use nanotechnology to increase equality throughout the world, or should nano-

tech be another way for the United States to maintain its global superiority? Are these goals mutually exclusive? Explain your reasoning.

2. Would Navrozov agree with Faunce and Nasu that nanotechnology weaponry should be subject to international regulation? Why or why not?

Organizations to Contact

The editors have compiled the following list of organizations concerned with the issues debated in this book. The descriptions are derived from materials provided by the organizations. All have publications or information available for interested readers. The list was compiled on the date of publication of the present volume; the information provided here may change. Be aware that many organizations take several weeks or longer to respond to inquiries, so allow as much time as possible.

American Nano Society (ANS)
e-mail: ans@nanosociety.us
website: www.nanosociety.us

The ANS is an international nonprofit organization dedicated to advancing nanotechnology. It functions as a professional society for academics and professional working in nanotechnology. It holds meetings, promotes education, and acts as a spokesperson for nanotechnology. It publishes *Nano Magazine* and the *Journal of the American Nano Society*, as well as books relating to nanotechnology. Its website also includes articles and news.

Center for Responsible Nanotechnology (CRN)
1379 Madera Ave., Menlo Park, CA 94025
(650) 776-5195
e-mail: info@crnano.org
website: www.crnano.org

The CRN is a nonprofit research and advocacy think tank concerned with the major societal and environmental implications of nanotechnology. It engages individuals and groups to better understand nanotechnology and to focus on its real risks and benefits. CRN's goal is to create and implement balanced plans for the responsible use of nanotechnology. Its website includes the *C-R-Newsletter*, press releases, policy statements, and a Nanotech Scenario series.

Foreseight Institute

Box 61058, Palo Alto, CA 94306
(650) 289-0860 • fax: (650) 289-0863
e-mail: foresight@foresight.org
website: www.foresight.org

The Foresight Institute is a think tank and public interest organization focused on transformative technologies. It works to discover and promote the benefits and help avoid the risks of nanotechnology, artificial intelligence, biotech, and similar technologies by educating the public, researchers, and policy makers. The institute publishes the monthly Foresight Institute *Update*, white papers, and briefing documents. Its website includes a blog, news updates, and articles.

Friends of the Earth Australia's Nanotechnology Project

PO Box 222, Fitzroy Victoria 3065
Australia
+61(0)435 589 579
website: http://nano.foe.org.au

Friends of the Earth is the world's largest federation of environmental organizations. The Nanotechnology project of the Australian branch takes a critical perspective on technology issues, focusing on the need for technologies to better reflect community needs and aspirations, not just commercial and military ones. The Nanotechnology Project publishes the newsletter *Nano News*, factsheets, and reports on its website.

The International Council on Nanotechnology (ICON)

Rice University, Houston, TX 77251
(214) 494-2071
website http://icon.rice.edu

ICON is an international organization whose mission is to develop and communicate information regarding potential environmental and health risks of nanotechnology in order to reduce those risks. ICON sponsors forums and events and provides an electronic data base for peer-reviewed nanotechnology articles. It publishes the *Virtual Journal of Nanotechnology Environment, Health, and Safety*, as well as reports, news and other information through its website.

Nanoethics Group
California Polytechnic State University
San Luis Obispo, CA 93407
(805) 756-1111
e-mail: hello@nanoethics.org
website: http://ethics.calpoly.edu

The Nanoethics Group is a research and education organization—not an advocacy, activist, or watchdog group. The Nanoethics Group is composed of professional ethicists with the scientific and business background to comment on issues in nanotechnology. The group works to approach nanotechnology with an open mind and to make complex issues understandable to the public. The website includes discussions of the group's work, links to media coverage, press releases, and links to papers and books by members of the group.

Nano Science and Technology Institute (NSTI)
3925 W. Braker Ln., Austin, TX 78759
(512) 692-7267 • fax: (925) 886-8461
e-mail: mlaudon@nsti.org
website: www.nsti.org

NSTI advances and integrates nano and other advanced technologies through education, conventions, business publishing, and research services. NSTI produces the annual Nanotech Conference and Expo. It publishes *Nanotech Conference Technical Proceedings*. Its website includes news, information about events, and other resources.

National Center for Nanoscience and Technology (NCNST)
No.ll ZhongGuanCun BeiYiTiao, Beijing 100190
P.R. China
+861 (0)825 45545 • fax:+861 (0)626 56765

e-mail: webmaster@nanoctr.cn
website: http://english.nanoctr.cas.cn

The NCNST is the Chinese government organization working on basic and applied research in nanoscience. Its website includes news, research, scientific papers, and other information on the center's work.

National Nanotechnology Initiative (NNI)
4201 Wilson Blvd., Stafford II, Rm. 405, Arlington, VA 22230
(703) 292-8626
e-mail: info@nnco.nano.gov
website: www.nano.gov

The NNI is a US government initative established as the central point of communication and collaboration for all federal agencies engaged in nanotechnology research. It publishes numerous publications and reports that can be downloaded from its website.

SAFENANO-Europe's Centre of Excellence on Nanotechnology Hazard and Risk
The Institute of Occupational Medicine, Research Avenue
North Riccarton, Edinburgh EH14 4AP
UK
+44(0)131 449 8003
e-mail: rob.aitken@safenano.org
website: www.safenano.org/

SAFENANO works to develop nanotechnology on a safe, sustainable and profitable basis. It brings together multidisciplinary expertise to provide occupational hygience and risk assessment and to responsibly develop safe nanomaterials. Its website includes information about research, safety guidelines, and numerous downloadable guides and documents.

Bibliography of Books

Chris Binns	*Introduction to Nanoscience and Nanotechnology*. Hoboken, NJ: Wiley & Sons, 2010.
Michael T. Burke	*Nanotechnology: The Business*. Boca Raton, FL: CRC Press, 2009.
Eric Drexler	*Engines of Creation: The Coming Era of Nanotechnology*. New York: Anchor Books, 1986.
Eric Drexler, Chris Peterson, and Gayle Pergamit	*Unbounding the Future: The Nanotechnology Revolution*. New York: Morrow/Quill, 1993.
Lynn E. Foster	*Nanotechnology: Science, Innovation, and Opportunity*. Upper Saddle River, NJ: Prentice Hall, 2005.
J. Storrs Hall	*Nanofuture: What's Next for Nanotechnology*. Amherst, NY: Prometheus Books, 2005.
Sean A. Hays, Jason Scott Robert, Clark A. Miller, and Ira Bennett, eds.	*Nanotechnology, The Brain, and the Future*. New York: Springer, 2013.
Richard A.L. Jones	*Soft Machines: Nanotechnology and Life*. New York: Oxford University Press, 2004.

Ahmed S. Khan	*Nanotechnology: Ethical and Social Implications*. Boca Raton, FL: CRC Press, 2012.
Margaret Kosal	*Nanotechnology for Chemical and Biological Defense*. New York: Springer, 2009.
W. Patrick McCray	*The Visioneers: How a Group of Elite Scientists Pursued Space Colonies, Nanotechnologies, and a Limitless Future*. Princeton, NJ: Princeton University Press, 2013.
Jeffrey T. Morris	*Risk, Language, and Power: The Nanotechnology Environmental Policy Case*. Lanham, MD: Lexington Books, 2012.
Robert V. Neumann	*Nanotechnology and the Environment*. Hauppauge, NY: Nova Science, 2010.
Susanna Hornig Priest	*Nanotechnology and the Public: Risk Perception and Risk Communication*. Boca Raton, FL: CRC Press, 2012.
Daniel Ratner and Mark A. Ratner	*Nanotechnology and Homeland Security: New Weapons for New Wars*. Upper Saddle River, NJ: Prentice Hall, 2004.
Ben Rogers, Sumita Pennathur, and Jesse Adams	*Nanotechnology: Understanding Small Systems*. 2nd ed. Boca Raton, FL: CRC Press, 2011.
Sanjeeb K. Sahoo	*Nanotechnology in Health Care*. Singapore: Pan Stanford, 2012.

Ted Sargent	*The Dance of the Molecules: How Nanotechnology Is Changing Our Lives*. New York: Avalon, 2006.
Kathleen Sellers et al.	*Nanotechnology and the Environment*. Boca Raton, FL: CRC Press, 2009.
Jo Anne Shatkin	*Nanotechnology: Health and Environmental Risks*. 2nd ed. Boca Raton, FL: CRC Press, 2013.
Geoffrey B. Smith and Claes-Goran S. Granqvist	*Green Nanotechnology: Solutions for Sustainability and Energy*. Boca Raton, FL: CRC Press, 2011.
Sherron Sparks	*Nanotechnology: Business Applications and Commercialization*. Boca Raton, FL: CRC Press, 2012.
Harry F. Tibbals	*Nanotechnology and Nanomedicine*. Boca Raton, FL: CRC Press, 2011.
Linda Williams and Wade Adams	*Nanotechnology Demystified*. New York: McGraw-Hill, 2007.
Edward L. Wolf and Manasa Medikonda	*Understanding the Nanotechnology Revolution*. Weinheim, Germany: Wiley-VCH, 2012.

Index

F

G

H

I

J

N

O

P

Q

R

S

V

W

Y

Z